PATIENCE

PATIENCE STRONG

PATIENCE STRONG

Tapestries of Time
Yesterdays and Tomorrows
The Magic of Memories

First published 1993 by Frederick Muller

This edition published in 1996 by SMITHMARK Publishers,
a division of U.S. Media Holdings, Inc.,
16 East 32nd Street, New York, NY 10016.

SMITHMARK books are available for bulk purchase
for sales promotion and premium use.
For details write or call the manager of special sales,
SMITHMARK Publishers, 16 East 32nd Street,
New York, NY 10016; (212) 532-6600.

Produced by Leopard, a division of Random House UK Ltd,
20 Vauxhall Bridge Road, London SW1V 2SA, UK

ISBN 0-7651-9655-7

Printed and bound in Great Britain

10 9 8 7 6 5 4 3 2 1

Contents

Tapestries
of
Time

Stepping Stones

Birthdays are like stepping stones –
    where Time's wide stream goes rushing by.
Sometimes in the sunlit shadows,
    sometimes in the deeps they lie . . .
But whether set in whirling pools
    or islanded in quietude,
we must stand and face the future
    in a high and happy mood.
Knowing God will take us forward
    if we trust Him without fear . . .
Every step a new adventure;
    every stone another year.

Morning Prayer

God bless my little home this day, before I start anew,
and guide my hands and give me strength for all I have to do.
May there be smiles and happy thoughts without a single tear
and no cross word creep in to mar the pleasant atmosphere.

And should some trifling thing go wrong to drag my spirits down
lift me above all petty strife and smooth away my frown.
And when the day is ended, I'll be waiting in my place
to welcome home my loved one with a calm and happy face.

Homeward Bound . . .

The City streets are dark with crowds – a moving, surging throng
All rushing, jostling eagerly, they press their way along . . .
And east and west and north and south from out the City's heart,
a million wheels are turning round, tubes, trains, trams – all a part

Of one great movement, streaming out, the countless faces blend
in one vast sea, yet each is turned towards its journey's end . . .
A single purpose drives them on – they meet on common ground
united in the urge for flight . . . The workers homeward bound.

Home

I try to make my home a place that's beautiful to see,
to fill each room with lovely things – and perfect harmony,
to polish up the copper pots, the silver and the brass,
and rub the walnut table till it gleams like crystal glass . . .
But home is not mere furniture.
The objects we see here are visible expressions of a wonderful
Idea –
a power that draws with ties of love wherever we may roam.
The centre of the universe and of the heart – the Home.

Tea-Time

I've invited my very best friend round to tea,
so the cakes must be golden and light . . .
I must see that there's plenty of fresh currant bread –
everything must be perfect, just right.
I shall use the blue china – the old willow set,
and the cloth with the ivory lace.
I shall put the chairs ready a whole hour before
and be waiting for her – in my place.
And my day will be full of excitement and fun,
but I know when it comes to an end,
there'll be only one memory left in my mind –
taking tea with my very best friend.

Grandfather Clock

There's a grandfather clock in the quiet old hall,
and it strikes with a deep-throated chime.
For he booms out the hours with a terrible voice,
and he cuts up our lives into Time.

He's a century old and he looks with disdain
on the folks who stare into his face.
For he knows that when their little lives flicker out,
he'll be still standing there in his place . . .

And he whirrs and he chuckles deep down in his works,
for he knows that we're all in his power
as, relentless, he roars out his challenge to men,
and he can't take back one single hour.

Gifts

Let us give and give again of all that we possess.
Not from the purse but from the heart – bright smiles and
                                                    kindliness,
the helping hand, the loving thought, the friendly word of praise,
encouraging some lonely soul through dark and stormy days . . .
The very poorest may be lavish with these lovely gifts.
Without a penny we may give the kindness that uplifts.
God never stints – He gives to men His riches from above.
Then may we give abundantly, the good gift of our love.

Listen!

'Listen' – that's a lovely word – it makes us quiet and still.
There's so much in the world to hear: the birds that chirp and trill;
the wild wind fluting in the trees; the drumming of the rain
the muffled fluttering of moths against a window pane:
Chopin, Beethoven, Liszt and Grieg – giants of music's art
created golden melodies to stir the human heart.

The world is full of lovely sounds – they fall about our ears.
Remembered in serenity, they echo down the years:
a voice we loved, a waterfall, a violin, a thrush,
all steal into the quiet heart in Memory's solemn hush . . .
So close your eyes and listen, you will hear all kinds of things –
the secret language of the flowers, the whirr of fairies' wings . . .

Shopping

It's fun to go shopping with someone you like –
some good friend who won't mind if you stop,
and you gaze in the windows and wander about
looking round in each different shop . . .

It's so nice just to stare at the things that you'd like,
though you haven't the money to buy –
pretty hats, shoes and gowns, books and furniture too,
lovely pictures – you have to pass by!

But I'm sure I'd be bored if I had all these things
for myself, heaps of money to spend,
for the wishing and wanting is half of the fun
of a day round the shops with a friend.

Fireside

The chairs are drawn around the fire – we gather round the blaze,
united in the fireside circle of the winter days.
The lamp is lit, the curtains drawn – and yet it's incomplete,
because the firelight shadows fall upon an empty seat . . .

Oh, please God, pity those who sit and face a vacant chair,
remembering the happy face – the loved one laughing there.
May He uplift them, give them strength to play their separate parts
and send His warmth to melt the frozen winter in their hearts . . .
Oh, may they feel the unseen presence of the one that's gone,
inspiring them with courage to be brave and carry on.

Broken Romance

You told me your story – a picture in words;
a garden with roses and sweet-singing birds;
and two lovers dreaming the moments away,
bewitched by the spell of the blue Summer's day . . .
A brief hour of magic and Love's ecstasies –
now locked in the casket of old memories.
The Summer has ended, the roses have gone,
the lovers have parted, yet Love lingers on.
The songs and the laughter have ended in tears,
as lonely, heartbroken they face the long years . . .
A sad little story, but who knows, my friend?
Your romance may still have a beautiful end.

Letters

The telephone has almost killed the sweet and gentle art
of writing lengthy letters, friend to friend, and heart to heart.
For people haven't got the time in this speed-crazy day
to put their thoughts on paper in a lovely, charming way . . .
To draw from wells of quiet thought, and set oneself apart,
to write a long, long letter from the fullness of the heart . . .
To take the pen and wander on down Memory's fragrant way,
reviving all the golden dreams of some sweet yesterday . . .

And so I keep my letters, tattered pages from the years.
They weave the story of the past with laughter, hope and tears.
They bridge the gulf from heart to heart. I read them all again,
and catch the quiet echoes of the rapture and the pain.

From a Window

The people who sit at a window and watch
as the crowds in the street pass along
see more than the people who rush to and fro
taking part in the big, noisy throng.
They get the best view of the things that occur
from the quiet of their hidden retreat,
while the folks who go pushing and jostling along
only see their small bit of the street . . .

It's the same in the swirl and chaos of life
when your world seems all frenzy and din –
just withdraw, and go into your own secret self;
looking out from the window within,
you will find that your troubles diminish and fade,
as remote as the far stars on high,
then serene in the stillness, your heart will grow wise
as you watch the mad world rushing by.

Cradles

I love to look at cradles, for they seem to symbolise
the whole of human tenderness; their pretty frills and ties
are emblems of the love that spreads its kind protective wings
around the helpless and the weak, and small defenceless things . .
And we are all defenceless from the moment of our birth –
frail, tiny figures strutting on our little spinning earth.
Our world is whirling in the void, we face Eternity –
We cannot probe the secrets of our hidden Destiny . . .

And yet we, too, are cradles, safe within His tender care.
The Love too deep for man to know is always waiting there –
creating, and controlling, suns and stars and worlds above.
And we are safe within the cradle of that perfect Love . . .

Slippers

I love to see a pair of slippers on the fireside mat.
It looks untidy, I'll admit, but who cares about that?
For slippers are so intimate, so nice and homely too,
especially when they're very old – I hate them when they're new!.

They seem to know they're waiting for two tired and weary feet.
I'm sure they hear their owners coming homeward down the
street . . .

Our shoes may look quite trim and smart as we go on our way,
but when we sit beside the fire and dream at close of day,
it's nice to take them off and slip our slippers on instead
– and let them take us quietly up the stairs, and so to bed.

Bedside Books

My house is full of well-loved books. They're scattered round
    the place –
in unexpected corners, on the shelves and in the case.
But on the table by my bed, I keep a little row
of precious books – my favourite ones – and when I'm tired I go
and find some passage that inspires with words like angel wings
that lift me up above the swirl of petty human things . . .
A truth from some great poet's pen, a lovely, lilting phrase –
a message that will spur me on, and light the darkest days.

Goodnight, Children

Goodnight, children! – and dream your happy dreams.
Forget your cares, forget your tears, and all your gallant schemes.
Tomorrow lies before you like an undiscovered land,
with shining possibilities – the lovely things you've planned
are blurred into a golden haze in which you play your part
in valiant adventures with a brave and fearless heart.

The rabbit and the kittens and the fishes in the streams,
the soldiers and the sugar mouse go marching through your dreams.
And though the darkness must descend, and toys be put away,
God always sends Tomorrow when He takes away Today.

Welcome

'Welcome' is a lovely word. It means so many things –
the warmth of human friendship and the pleasure that it brings;
true greetings of the kindly hearts who share what they possess;
the cheery hearth, the cosy home – and joy and happiness . . .
For hospitality does not depend upon our store.
It's what we mean by 'Welcome' when our friends are at the door

The Spare Room

It's only just a little room with simple, homely things.
The only sound comes from the eaves, the sound of tiny wings.
The boards are stained a shining brown, the walls are painted
cream –
a simple room, a quiet room, in which to sleep and dream . . .

I like to peep inside the door and take it unawares,
to see the oaken bedstead and the little wicker chairs.
And then, in some mysterious way, I feel the room is blessed.
Whoever sleeps within its walls will find a perfect rest.

It offers to the restless heart a hospitality
that's warm and rich because it springs from real simplicity.

And in this humble little room its meaning is expressed –
the blessing of the presence of the well-beloved guest.

Roofs

I love to climb the hill that lies behind our little town.
And when the sun shines after rain, it's lovely to look down
upon the little coloured roofs, lit by the sun's bright ray –
a beautiful mosaic, brown and red and green and grey . . .

The town looks small and toy-like underneath the sky's great do
and as I gaze, I realise that each roof is a home
where people strive and work and play, and children laugh and c
and men and women play their parts, and live and love and die .

And yet the town looks so content, so happy and serene,
with all its little shining roofs of red and brown and green.
And as the daylight fades to dusk, I watch as sunset gleams,
and pray God sends to every home joy, peace, and happy dream

Sleep

Sleep is a soft and gentle hand that charms away all strife,
and draws us with a magic touch from out the grasp of Life.
It throws into our tired eyes, the golden dust of dreams.
And we forget our failures and our little futile schemes . . .

If you've a grievance in your heart, don't rail and storm and weep,
just put a finger on the lips and then lie down and sleep.
And in the morning when you wake, you'll take a different view –
for God gives you another day in which to start anew.

Alarm-Clock

When we are sleeping in our beds, the grim, relentless clock
starts ringing loudly in our ears and gives us such a shock.
It says, 'Come on, you lazy thing, and don't you hesitate.
There's work to do, you know the time, so don't dare be late!'

Oh, how we hate that cruel clock, especially when we're cold.
We have to leave our cosy beds and do just as we're told,
and face the bleak realities that crowd upon the mind –
begin the day and leave our rosy dreamland far behind.

And Life's like that – we think that we're secure and safe and warm
and suddenly we find we've got to face the strife and storm.
Some trouble comes along and gives us such a nasty knock.
Just like the rude awakening of that fiendish thing – the Clock!

Jealousy

He looks at Baby Peter with his sad and mournful eyes.
He doesn't understand things, and his thoughts he can't disguise.
He used to be the petted darling of the family,
and now he takes a second place – that's plain enough to see!
For years he was their own devoted pal, and then one day
a tiny stranger came to town. Imagine his dismay!
His master and his mistress did their best to make amends,
and show him that the four of them could be the greatest friends.

He wags his tail and gives a sniff and tries to raise a smile,
although his faithful doggie heart is breaking all the while,
because he knows that things can never never be the same.
The world is turned all upside down – since Baby Peter came.

Potpourri

Pretty painted china bowl upon the window sill –
I love to catch the sweet elusive perfume you distil.
It steals upon me in the greyness of the twilight hours –
the half-forgotten fragrance of the lovely summer flowers . . .

I close my eyes, and when this sweetness hangs upon the air,
the winter scene is blotted out – I see a garden fair,
with roses, pinks and lavender, with mignonette and musk,
and all the beauty of a garden in a summer dusk . . .

I wish I could preserve my happy memories like this –
the dreams of youth, the golden hopes, the hours of perfect bliss.
All gathered up like petals, stored away, and set apart,
hidden in the secret places of a quiet heart.

Old Age

Old Age never comes to us when Youth is in the mind.
When we have left the wild, ecstatic days of Spring behind,
we come upon a richer time of deep content and peace,
when all the heart's red wounds are healed, and our rebellions
cease . . .
When quiet hours bring memories that steal from out the years –
and lift us up on wings of dreams, and sorrow disappears.
And only happiness remains from all the crowded past,
if we have gathered to ourselves the things that really last.

The body may be broken, but the mind may still expand
and touch the rosy fringes of that good and better Land . . .
The spirit is forever young. Unfettered it can rise
and probe the secrets of the wind, the stars, the trees, the skies . . .
The old may go adventuring to seek the heart's desire
and live a thousand lives again when dreaming by the fire.

Happy Trio

Baby, Mother, Grandmamma – the trio is complete.
Three happy people. Life for them is good and very sweet.
For Grandma finds fulfilment in her daughter's perfect joy.
And mother has her first-born child – a little baby boy . . .

Oh, may the years be very kind, no tears and fears and frowns.
Yet changes come, babies grow up. Life is all ups and downs.
But may you cling together as you go the winding way –
and be a happy little trio, as you are today.

Happy Home

I read your note, my friend, and I can picture where you live.
A happy home – what more on earth can God in heaven give?
A cottage nestling in the trees, a place of peace and rest,
made perfect by a love that's true – our home is surely blessed . . .

I see the red brick fireplace, and the brass all shining bright.
I see the pretty curtains that you draw in every night.
Oh may you keep it as it is – paradise for two,
where fondest hopes are satisfied, and all your dreams come true.

Home Sweet Home

Home may be a castle or a villa or a cot.
No matter if it's grand or small – it is a sacred spot,
where we can come when we are tired of Life's mad circus show,
of shams and empty pleasures blindly rushing to and fro.
And seeking for the happiness that Home alone can give,
God give us quiet and simple hearts and teach us how to live!

A home may be an anchor in the troubled storms of life,
a refuge from this world of pain and selfishness and strife . . .
To welcome us at any time wherever we may roam –
four walls around a universe that men call Home Sweet Home.

Pie-Crust

Pie-crust looks so nice and firm, and yet it always breaks.
It's made just to be crumbled into little bits and flakes.
And oh, how many promises are broken in this way –
made in an idle moment, and forgotten the next day!
Think well before you make a promise. Keep it if you do,
or you will find that people will lose confidence in you.
Somebody counts upon your word, so don't betray their trust.
A promise is a promise, not a little bit of crust . . .
Why wait until tomorrow? Now's the time – don't be deterred.
In big things or in trifles – we must keep our word.

Christening

'What shall we call him?' Mother asked. 'The christening's today.
We must make up our minds – I really don't know what to say . . .
The aunties and the uncles will be here at half-past three.
And Father's name must come into it – whatever shall it be?

Patrick, David, Stephen, John – they're all so very nice.
If only he could speak to us and give us his advice!
No matter what our choice may be, God bless my baby's name.
And though it may not bring us glory, wealth or worldly fame,
oh, may it be remembered for the things of highest worth –
for all the splendid things that really matter on this earth –

straight dealing and good sportsmanship, high standards and fair
play:
the name that we shall give our little baby boy today
. . . A name to honour and respect, and when Life's shadows fall,
he'll realise a good name is the greatest thing of all.'

Cottage Garden

What could be more lovely on a golden summer day
than this old cottage garden somewhere Surrey way.
Lupins like bright candles burning in the sultry air.
Poppies like red wisps of paper in the sun's fierce glare.
Pansies dreaming by the borders – wide-eyed, in a trance.
Boughs of apple shuffling shadows where the sunbeams dance.
Butterflies with powdered wings and drowsy droning bees.
Scent of full-blown cabbage roses drifting on the breeze.
Passionflowers that fall across the lattice in a shower.
Who am I, dear God, that I should have this perfect hour?

Decisions

We reach the parting of the ways, and then we must decide
which pathway we shall take – it's hard, we have no human guide.
Each road is dark and unexplored. We face the great unknown –
and in that final moment everyone must stand alone . . .

So much may hang upon a word. So many things at stake –
careers, and lives and happiness, and in the choice we make
we spin the webs of destiny for good or ill. And so
when you're perplexed and cannot see the way in which to go,

be still and wait for guidance and you will not wait in vain –
no need for panic or distress, no need to strive and strain . . .
Trust with a quiet confidence. You'll know the thing to do,
and you will hear the voice of Wisdom at the heart of you.

Homecoming

Coming home – the very words turn grey skies into blue.
Coming home . . . O happy thought! For life begins anew.
Hands stretched out in welcome from the homely little door,
things in their accustomed place, just as they were before.
Tables, carpets, books and chairs all smile as if they knew
that Mother's coming home today. They share the secret too.

It's lonely in the dear old home without her smiling face.
Her absence makes it seem a very dreary kind of place.
But now the longed-for day has come. She's coming home again –
forgotten all the anxious hours of worry and of pain . . .
God bless the sweet reunion of this happy family –
and grant Thy peace and happiness through all the years to be.

Long-Distance Call

A voice was borne across the sea
to greet a happy family;
imagine their surprise when they
could hear their loved one far away . . .
The dear familiar voice came through,
reviving memories anew,
and they'll recall in years to be
that voice across the distant sea.

This is the wonder of our day –
that from a thousand miles away
a voice could travel on a beam.
It's like the magic of a dream!
It brings our friends back home again,
without the aid of ship or train.
It brings them close, though seas divide –
it is as if they're at our side . . .
The lonely hours have never been.
A voice can bridge the years between.
Goodbye is robbed of all its pain.
It's so long – till we phone again.

Lovers' Lane

It's lovely in the summer days – a perfect lovers' lane.
It's shady in the sunshine and it's fragrant in the rain;
the wild flowers in the hedges fling their perfume on the breeze.
From dawn to dusk the birds trill out their music in the trees . . .
When day is ended and the world is wrapped in evening's calm,
the lovers down the leafy lane go strolling arm in arm;
they dream Love's gay romantic dreams, exploring magic realms,
until the moon comes peeping through the tangle of the elms . . .

Then homeward to the village where the lighted windows gleam,
enchanted in the secret rapture of a lover's dream . . .
What ardent hopes are harboured in the heart of man and maid!
The common earth is holy ground when, brave and unafraid,
they view from youth's high peak of faith the years that are to be –
and heart to heart they make their vows for all Eternity . . .

Oh, may they never lose this sense of magic and delight
that clings about them as they walk, enraptured, through the night.
No matter what the years may hold of pleasure or of pain,
may life for them be one long stroll along lover's lane.

Picnic

It's fun to have a picnic on a lovely summer's day
in some green meadow where a little river winds its way;
a fragrant bank where willows trail their branches gracefully.
It's nice to have a party underneath a kind old tree . . .
To spread the cloth upon the grass, and set the plates around;
to drink your tea and eat your cakes while seated on the ground –
fat doughnuts, jam and creamy buns, and things that normally
you really wouldn't dream of eating with your cup of tea!
Your fingers may be sticky, but that's half the fun of it,
the wasps may settle in the jam, but you won't care a bit!

But when you've had your picnic, don't forget to make the place
exactly as you found it, leaving not a single trace . . .
For if, for instance, you were asked to tea with friends next door –
you wouldn't leave a lot of litter lying on the floor,
now would you? And it's just the same in Nature's lovely bowers.
She's so hospitable and kind – she gives us fields and flowers,
and shady nooks by babbling brooks, where we can take our ease,
and have a picnic underneath the shelter of the trees.

Reliability

When you make a promise, keep it, trifling though it be.
Win a reputation for reliability.
Never go back on your word or disappoint your friends.
Don't do something mean and weak, then rush to make amends.

Can you be relied upon to carry through a plan?
Can you be relied upon to do the best you can?
Are you to be trusted in some great emergency?
Can you take the weight of a responsibility?

Fickle folks draw fickle friends, and many friends mean none.
In this world we're truly lucky if we find but one.
One faithful friend that needs no vow, no gift, no bribe, no tie.
One true and dear and trusted friend on whom we may rely . . .

And such a friend comes not by chance. Life's laws are good
                                                     and just,
for friendship such as this is built on honour, faith and trust.

Birthday Flowers

Whether your birthday season comes
    with autumn's rich chrysanthemums,
or with the winter's frosty air
    when blooms are scarce and flowers are rare,
or if your introduction here
    was in the springtime of the year,
your favourites are those, I'd say,
    which greet you on your natal day,
saying, Many happy hours,
    in the language of the flowers.

Time

Life's a gamble. Life's a scramble. Fret and turmoil, strife and noise.
Life's a worry. What's the hurry? Give me peace and quiet joys.

Life's all clamour; fake and glamour, tinsel shams and vulgar show;
fight for money. Aren't folks funny? Rushing madly to and fro.

Give me leisure; simple pleasure; time in which to stand and stare.
Time to wonder; time to wander; time to dream; and time to spare.
Time for gazing; time for raising weary eyes to leaf and wing;
time for praying; time for saying: Thank You, God, for everything.

The Happy Day

Let this be a happy day –
all the while and all the way.
May the dearest dream come true,
and the best be granted you . . .
Good friends to your door be sent,
and your heart be well content
with what the day may leave behind.
Time be good and Life be kind.

Life's the Thing

Life's the thing – so be alive and always look alive,
whether you are seventeen or rising seventy-five.
It's not the length of years that counts; it is the quality
that determines what kind of a living yours is going to be . . .
There's no generation gap. Age is illusory.
Life's the thing. Enjoy it, love it, live it gloriously.

Bereavement

Sorrow comes unto the door of every family.
Changes come as loved ones go. That's life. It has to be . . .
The empty future looms ahead. A blank we have to face.
In the heart there is a silence and a vacant place.

Death breaks up the old familiar pattern of the days.
We have to work a new one out in unaccustomed ways.
At first it seems impossible, but when we've dried our tears
we see another pattern being traced out through the years.

Content

Content I pray I'll always be
with home and hearth and family . . .
Content in my small realm to reign.
Happy in my own domain.

Thankful for whatever's there,
though it be but frugal fare . . .
Every meal a sacrament
when the spirit is content.

Content with what comes to my door.
Not always wanting something more.
But grateful for the odds and ends
that a God of mercy sends.

When Troubles Come

When troubles come we find our truest friends.
The knowledge of their affection lends
a glow to gloom, a cheering, warming ray
that helps us face the darkness of the day.

The word that heartens and the kindly thought
give us courage, comfort and support . . .
If we have proved a friend to somebody,
we too find friendship in adversity.

Something That Belonged to Mother

Often when I'm looking for a thing I have mislaid,
I come on some forgotten odds and ends. Time seems to fade,
and in a flash leap across the years because I see
things that stab my heart awake with Mother's memory.

A photograph, some beads, a thimble, kept I know not why –
a sentimental whim has always made me put them by;
and so they keep on turning up to haunt me through the years.
It's foolish, but I cling to them – these little souvenirs.

This Lovely Memory

Dear, let us remember this when we are tired and old –
When we sit beside the fire and days are drear and cold.
Let us warm our hearts against this lovely memory –
keeping it forever bright through all the years to be.
Drifting on the river in a dream world of our own;
gliding through enchanted country, you and I alone . . .
Sunlit waters rippling by and willows up above –
two young people whispering the old, old words of love.

Say you never will forget this golden afternoon.
Time will bring its changes and the winter comes too soon . . .
Say you will remember when the gold has turned to grey –
Let us keep unto the end the dream we've dreamed today.

Just Kindness

Kindness, just kindness is all that it takes
to make a day happy, for kindliness makes
for peace and for cheerfulness, grace and goodwill,
stirring no trouble, and speaking no ill.

Feeling for others and trying to ease
the burden that presses, to help and to please;
forgetting yourself and your own heavy load;
thinking of somebody else on the road.

The value of kindness you cannot assess.
Spoken or written no word can express
how one little kindness can make someone's day –
giving him courage to go on his way,
a smile on his lips and a song in his mind,
just because somebody somewhere was kind.

Give Me the Simple Things of Life

Give me the simple things of life: a cottage hearth, a quiet room,
a little garden green with trees, where birds make song midst leaf
  and bloom.

Give me the happy things of life: a heart that's merry all the way,
an outlook that is broad and bright, a spirit that is brave and gay.

Give me the lasting things of life: a faith that nothing can destroy
the kindly company of friends, and love to crown my days with j

Time Alone

Time alone can make a garden, giving it the mellow tones
of the lichen and the moss that stain the worn and weathered
stones . . .
Only old well-rooted trees can spread their branches thick and
wide,
casting long and lovely shadows on the lawns at eventide.

Man can plan and plant and work it – but it is the years that bring
growth and glory in their train and leave their mark on everything.
Time alone can give that touch that makes a garden fair to see,
rounding off the edges with the beauty of maturity.

The Blessing

The blessing of a loving mother nobody can measure.
You cannot put it into words or price this precious treasure . . .
She suffers when you suffer and she shares in your success.
She works for you and wishes for your health and happiness.

Your love express in words before she passes on her way –
then there'll be no sadness over what you failed to say . . .
It is now that kindness counts; we sometimes leave too late
a thank you for some little thing that we appreciate.

Always Young

I'm always young while you are here.
You are my childhood, mother dear.
You are my youth. Your smiling face
comes haunting every secret place
within the caves of memory;
for you were always there with me
in all those wonderful events
of the years of innocence
when the sun shone every day.
Or so it seemed; all fun and play.
Life was one long lovely Spring.
There was a bloom on everything.

While you're still near I catch the glow
reflected from the long ago.
Stay, dear Mother. Never go.

Mother of the Bride

She has played her part and now there's nothing to be done –
but play the charming hostess with a smile for everyone . . .
There she is, a radiant figure, elegant and smart,
although we know just how she must be feeling in her heart.

For her, as well as for her girl, it is the day of days.
She knows it is a milestone and the ending of a phase.
But ends are new beginnings where the roads of life divide.
So Time be kind, and may God bless the Mother of the bride.

Happy Morning

Greet the day with happy heart and vow that it will be
a well-lived and a worthwhile day. Accept it gratefully
as a good and precious gift, a newly given chance
to wrest a blessing out of every twist of circumstance.

Grey the day may look to you when first you wake to it.
Don't go by appearance. Later on it may be lit
with sunny gleams and golden dreams, adventure and romance.
You must not judge a day by what it looks like at a glance.

Even though the day holds out no hope of happiness,
don't despise it or despair for you can never guess
what it may unfold before the sunset dies away.
Greet with glad thanksgiving the beginning of each day.

Make a Rainbow

If your world looks gloomy and you're feeling grim and glum,
make a rainbow for yourself, don't wait for one to come.
Don't sit watching at the window for the clouds to part.
There'll soon be a rainbow if you start one in your heart.

Take some lovely thought out of a poem or a prayer.
Turn it over in your mind and let it linger there.
Keep out every memory that dims the light within,
and hold on to the magic word that lets the brightness in.

Work your own small miracle and make the dull days glow.
Put some sunshine into life and let the glory show.
Make a rainbow for yourself with colours brave and gay,
and underneath its golden arch your cares will fade away.

Our Dancing Years

It is only a melody recalled from long ago,
but it has the power to set my empty heart aglow
with memories that go back to the rich romantic past,
when love was new and life was good; so good – too good to last.

It is only a melody upon a record played,
but it fills the room with pictures that can never fade,
more vivid and more real than those that hang upon the wall.
How wonderful that this small disc can resurrect it all
with such a deep intensity,
and bring you laughing back to me
without the hurt, without the tears,
to live again our dancing years.

Too Late Now

When you come we meet as friends, but when you say goodbye,
you leave a haunting sadness like the echo of a sigh . . .
Merry is the laughter, gay the talk and bright the scene,
but underneath it all I hear the words: it might have been.

Yes, indeed, it might have been. I see it in your eyes.
We might have loved each other once – but things went otherwise
Life works out its own designs, and we survive somehow.
All is for the best, they say. Too late for loving now . . .
Too late for disentangling the frayed and twisted thread;
too late to obliterate the foolish words we said.
For a different kind of life the stage has now been set.
Burden not the present with the ashes of regret.

Gardens Bring Back Memories

Gardens bring back memories, the thought of bygone hours
mingles with the present as you walk amongst your flowers . . .
They stir the recollection of some unforgotten place,
and call to mind out of the past, a scene, a voice, a face.

Even when the last rose falls upon the frosted clay,
you catch upon the wintry wind a song of yesterday.
In every corner of the garden something you will see
that evokes within your heart some lovely memory.

Time Will Bring It Back

No good deed is ever wasted and no kind word said in vain
for the good we do for others, life brings back to us again . . .
Every seed of love you sow will spring up somewhere on the road
and the sacrifice you make will serve to lighten someone's load.

No good deed is lost to God although it may be lost to view.
Cast your bread upon the waters. Time will bring it back to you.

A Window Looking West

I love a room that has a window looking to the west.
Morning has its glories, but it's this I love the best:
the evening view that opens at the gold end of the day,
when the sun goes down in pearly clouds of rose and grey.

At the day's beginning sunny windows we must shun.
Life comes rushing in and there are duties to be done . . .
No one has the time to sit and watch the spectacle
of the dawn that makes the world all fresh and beautiful.

But when the doors are closed upon the busy crowded days,
it is good to have a room where you can turn your gaze
to the quiet landscapes of the view you love the best
through the golden casements of a window looking west.

Lose Yourself

Lose yourself with all your wants, your worry and your woe.
Lose yourself in other people's troubles. Yours will go . . .
Lose yourself by getting lost in someone else's maze –
helping one another through the dark unhappy days.

Lose yourself in something bigger than your own affairs.
Lose yourself, immersed in all the problems and the cares
that surround you day by day. You'll soon forget your own –
for you'll come to realise that you are not alone,
suffering in isolation; others suffer too.
Lose yourself to find yourself and when at last you do,
you will find a better person than you were before,
when you lived for self alone behind your own front door.

Not Easy

It's not always easy to hold your tongue when people are unkind.
It's not always easy to walk away and put it from your mind –
but quarrelling never put anything right, it seems to make things
  worse,
and leaves you with a hornet's nest of grievances to nurse.

It's not always easy to turn aside and show the other cheek,
because you're afraid they will think that you are spiritless and
  weak . . .
No, it's not easy but it's the only thing to do you'll find –
if you want to keep your friendships and your peace of mind.

A Friend

A friend is someone who will always try to understand,
one in whom you can confide when things get out of hand . . .
Someone who will listen when by bad luck you've been hit,
never offering advice unless you ask for it.

So grapple him, said Shakespeare, to your heart with hoops of
  steel.
Lonely you will never be and helpless never feel,
if you have a friend like this when crosses you must bear.
You may not meet for months, but when he's needed . . . he'll
  be there.

I Walked in Memory Lane Today

I walked in Memory Lane today.
It was roses all the way,
until I heard a voice that said:
Turn back. Walk not the path ahead.

But on I pressed till suddenly
thorns and nettles tortured me . . .
My fingers bled, my sleeve was rent,
as down the tangled track I went.

Go not too often or too far
along the road where memories are,
but find content and pleasures new
in what the present holds for you.

Take What Comes

Don't expect perfection for you'll never find it here.
This is earth, not heaven, so with charity and cheer
take what comes – the good, the bad, and don't start whimpering
when you're disappointed with a person or a thing.

Do not worship idols and complain when you have found
feet of clay beneath the robes in which you've wrapped them
round . . .
Everyone is human. Do not be too critical
when someone fails, Remember that you, too, are fallible.

Keep your ideals in your heart and set your standard high,
but don't lose faith when things go wrong. Just let the storm
blow by . . .
Do not ask too much of life or reach beyond your range.
Accept and learn to live content with what you cannot change.

One by One

You do not have to take in one great stride
the busy day that lies ahead of you.
When troubles loom around on every side,
and nowhere can you see a clear way through.
Just take it step by step and you will find
fears fade like snowflakes melting in the sun . . .
The worst things happen only in the mind,
and problems are disposed of one by one.

So Little

The gentle smile, the reconciling touch
can cost so little and can mean so much –
to heal a breach or mend a friendship broken,
a letter written, or a sentence spoken.

What hurts and pangs we suffer needlessly!
What pains inflict, because we cannot see
how much we lost through conflicts and contentions,
poisoning life with quarrels and dissensions.

Let them all go and love triumphant be
over all evil, hate, greed, jealousy . . .
Love's tender word, forbearing and forgiving,
brings to the heart true peace and joy of living.

Cosiness

Some folks yearn for luxury, for grand and costly things –
but I prefer the homely touch; a cosy room that brings
a warming glow into the heart, a room that seems to say,
'Come right in and welcome,' on a cold and gloomy day.

These are the things that give a place a snug and friendly air:
the gleam of oak and brass and copper and a chintzy chair.
A bowl of flowers, a shelf of books, a softly shaded light.
And a little casement hung with curtains gay and bright.

A firelit ingle and a kettle singing merrily.
A pile of logs upon the hearth – the table set for tea.
Who would wish for what is showy and magnificent?
These are the things that make for comfort and for sweet content.

The Instrument

Play life like an instrument, making melodies.
Change the daily discords into harmonies . . .
Draw the sweetness from it. Somebody may hear
the tune behind the strident sounds that jar upon the ear.
Make your music as you move through the world's distress.
Someone passing by may catch your note of happiness . . .
Play life gently, play it softly. Play with style and grace –
bringing beauty out of what is dull and commonplace.

Happiness Waiting for You

There is light at the end of the tunnel.
There is calm at the end of the storm . . .
There is rest at the end of the journey,
and a hearth that is welcome and warm.

There's a star on the top of the mountain
you can touch when the last crag is scaled.
There's a certain reward for the faithful
at the point where they think they have failed.

There's a spring at the end of the winter
and behind the black cloud it is blue . . .
There's a song at the heart of your sorrow,
and happiness waiting for you.

Give Your Love

Give your love to others. Don't spend it on yourself.
Give your heart's good treasure. Don't hoard it on the shelf . . .
Give a word of comfort. Give a helping hand.
Give where it is needed. Try to understand.

Give the best that's in you to the job you do.
Give the world your blessing and it blesses you . . .
Give your life to something that is well worthwhile.
Give – and never ever forget to give a smile.

The Best in Life

The best and sweetest things in life are things you cannot buy:
the music of the birds at dawn, the rainbows in the sky;
the dazzling magic of the stars, the miracle of light;
the precious gifts of health and strength, of hearing, speech and
                                                              sight;

the peace of mind that crowns a busy
life of work well done; a faith in God
that deepens as you face the setting sun;
the pearl of love, the gems of friendship.
As the years go by
you find the greatest blessings are the things you cannot buy.

If the Heart Is Singing

If the heart is singing you cannot go far wrong –
for you will discover there's magic in a song
that scares away the demons that throng around us all,
wanting us to stumble and to see us fall.

If the heart is singing nothing can get through –
only that which strengthens and what is best for you.

Let the world go grumbling and grinding on its way,
for you'll have the secret that lights the common day.
You'll see the hidden glory behind the leaden cloud.
Lightly you will travel, head high and back unbowed,
for when the heart is singing the soul is singing too.
Your sins will be forgiven, for every day is new.

As Roses Have Thorns

As roses have thorns, so does love have its times
    of testings, frustrations and pains.
But what is it worth if it cannot withstand
    the pressures, the heartaches and strains?

Love's depths can't be measured by kiss, word or gift –
    but by sympathy tender and true;
the will to forbear, to forgive,
to forget, and to take the most generous view –
hiding the scars and the stings that still smart,
ready to laugh and to make a new start.

Happy House

Is this a happy house? Yes. You will know
once you have stepped inside. Faces will show
that sort of happiness none can disguise.
It's in the smile of the lips and the eyes.

Is this a happy house? Yes, if Love here
makes its abiding and dwells year by year . . .
Love's quiet presence is sensed and is heard
in helpfulness, kindness and courteous words.

Is this a happy house? Yes, if so be –
somebody prays in it. Prayer secretly
sweetens and brightens wherever it's said,
and calls down a blessing on every head.

The Haven of the Heart

I never cease to find it strange
how in a flash the world can change . . .
Things can happen overnight,
and suddenly it all comes right.

Life may not go the way you planned.
You cannot hope to understand the hidden hand
of Providence
that works unseen behind events.
But patience waits to serve her turn,
and if on faith you lean, you learn
to live by truths not understood,
that lead at last unto the good
that you have sought unconsciously;
the haven where your heart would be.

Somebody's Tomorrow

Is anyone the happier for meeting you today?
Has anyone been prayed for just because he came your way?
Has anyone been helped because you stopped to lend a hand,
spared a little time to listen, tried to understand?

Has anyone been made to feel that God was somewhere near?
Has someone somewhere been relieved of worry and of fear?
Has someone rediscovered faith in what is good and true –
seen another side to life, another point of view?

If the answer's Yes, then you have earned your night's repose.
If no, your day was wasted, spent in vain, and at its close
there can be no satisfaction; not unless you say
that somebody's tomorrow will be better than today.

Together Again

Now we're together once more, we two.
The past we will bury and start anew,
making the best of what years remain,
mending our marriage, beginning again.

Wiser for every mistake we made,
letting unhappy memories fade,
thankful for having this second chance
to pick up the threads of the old romance.

Forward we'll look to the days ahead,
forgetting the things we did and said.
So foolish! Now everything's marvellous.
The future is ours and it's up to us.

A Promise

Keep a promise to a child whatever it may be.
Never ever break your word, but keep it faithfully . . .
Disappointments hurt the children, giving needless pain.
Once you let them down they won't believe in you again.

If you want your children to be honest, straight and true,
never give them cause to lose their confidence in you.
Set them an example. Always stand by what you've said.
Don't sow doubts or start suspicions in a little head.

Children have long memories. They bank on what you say.
Don't raise hopes then dash them with the words, 'Some other day
Once you've made a promise let them see that you are tied.
Teach them that it's something that you must not set aside.

Heart or Head

My heart is saying: This is love. But can it really be?
My heart is saying: This is it. It says you're meant for me . . .
But how, I wonder, can I tell if this is truly so.
Can the wayward heart be trusted? How am I to know?

Common sense says: Wait awhile. Don't risk a big mistake.
Pause before you start to think about a wedding cake . . .
Look before you take a final leap into the blue.
But my heart says, 'Fiddlesticks!' So what am I to do?

I admit that in the past I've often been misled.
But now it comes to this: am I to follow heart or head?
I ought to heed the voice that says it can't be genuine,
and yet I have a feeling that my heart is going to win.

Let Love Speak

Let the word of peace be spoken,
when relationships are broken.
Let Love speak and heal the smart
of wounds inflicted on the heart.

Let Love's language, sweet and tender,
its own gentle service render –
saying what is kind and wise,
with the lips or with the eyes.

Let no grievance leave an ember
that perhaps you may remember,
and regret in later years,
with your penitential tears.

Try forgiving. Try confessing.
Let Love speak the final blessing,
casting every doubt away,
before the closing of the day.

Ideal Home

It doesn't have to have the latest kitchen gadgetry,
central heating or a fridge. Nor does it need to be
like an illustration in a glossy magazine,
all complete with television and a wash-machine.

You can have the ideal home without these odds and ends,
if you have the things on which true happiness depends:
the comfort and companionship of friends and family,
centred round a hearth where there is peace and harmony.

These things make the ideal home and work the miracle.
The touch that turns the commonplace into the beautiful.
The love that lights the daily round and brightens every part.
The sunshine of good humour and the kindness of the heart.

Boy & Girl Affair

When you fall in love around the age of seventeen,
everything looks wonderful and wears a rosy sheen . . .
It's as if you're in a bubble floating through the clouds,
drifting in a rainbow-world away above the crowds.

It seldom lasts, that first romance . . . but treat it tenderly:
this morning madness of the heart, this April ecstasy . . .
This Springtime of experience when life is fresh and sweet
that comes upon you unawares and sweeps you off your feet.

Years will pass and it will be forgotten utterly –
then some day, one day, something will revive the memory,
like a sudden breath of blossoms on the wintry air,
and you'll remember once again that boy and girl affair.

Condolence

A few brief words I'm sending you in all sincerity,
to assure you of my deep and heartfelt sympathy . . .
When sorrows come to those we love we know not what to say,
words are so inadequate our feelings to convey.

None can really share our griefs. We suffer each apart,
for only God can speak the word that mends a broken heart.
Only He can give the peace that makes the soul resigned.
Only Time can bring the balm that calms the troubled mind.

All that I can do is pray that you'll be given power,
and the strength that you will need in this your bitter hour . . .
Words, I know, can't take away the pain another bears,
but I'm wanting you to know you're in my thoughts and prayers.

Pictures in the Fireside

What do you see in the fire tonight?
I see the oddest things:
A castle on a mountain-top
A bird with flaming wings.
An old man, a gnome I think,
A dwarf with pointed beard,
A cottage with three chimney pots.
A forest, wild and weird.
I see a ruby-studded cave,
With crimson stalactites.
And just behind that bit of coal
There are the strangest sights.
A lady with a basket
And a small boy with a dog.
Can't you see them seated there
Upon the apple log?

When I Remember You

I remember a thousand things when I remember you:
the firelight glowing on polished oak; a table set for two . . .
The gleam of lamps in a rain-washed street; the shimmer of wet
leaves.
The smoky grey of November nights. The blue of April eves.

A meeting under a station clock. A song, a smile, a dance.
The muted sweetness of violins; the music of romance . . .
A country walk and a cottage tea; a window with a view.
I remember a thousand things when I remember you.

Sharing

If we share we multiply the good things we possess.
If we share them we increase our joy and happiness . . .
If we cast our bread upon the stream of life's affairs
it may feed some hungry soul, or answer someone's prayers . . .
Time will bear it back to us, returning it will bring
a blessing and a joy unknown to those who clutch and cling
to what the good God give to them, the silver and the gold.
Things are only lent to us; they are not ours to hold.

If you hoard you block the channels. Let the good things flow.
Take with grateful joy the riches that the fates bestow.
Keep them not for selfish ends until the chance has gone.
Help to make God's gifts go round . . . and pass the blessings on

Fireside Rendezvous

Dream-faces from the shadows smile at me,
when from the busy world I draw apart . . .
Ghosts cross the threshold of my memory
as I unlatch the doorways of the heart.

Draw the bright curtains on the twilight gloom.
Shut out the darkness as the night descends . . .
Here in the silence of this firelit room
I have a rendezvous with absent friends.

Think

Think before you cut the link that snaps the golden chain –
Pause before you take a step that causes others pain . . .
Wait before you speak the word that tears old bonds apart –
Listen to the voice of conscience in your secret heart.

Think before you cast aside affection tried and true,
and break the faith of someone who has loved and trusted you.

Try a Little Humour

Try a little humour when life's going wrong.
Try a little laughter, try a little song . . .
It will work like magic when you're feeling low –
make a little effort, and the mood will go.

Try a little sunshine on a gloomy day.
Practise painting rainbows on a sky of grey . . .
Don't sit at the window grumbling at the showers –
weave a thread of brightness through the dreary hours.

Do not be despondent when the shadows fall.
Brooding on your problems will not help at all . . .
Fight down the depression and your feelings hide.
Try a little humour, see the funny side.

Open the Window

Open the window and let in the sun.
The season of life and of light has begun.
Open the window. The wind is a broom
that sweeps out the cobwebs, the dust and the gloom.

Open the windows of hope. Fling them wide,
when it is cheerless and stuffy inside . . .
Germs of self-pity, of fear and of doubt
thrive in the darkness, so drive them all out.

Viewed from the shadows through windows shut fast,
the future is veiled in the fogs of the past . . .
But eyes that can see with a faith big and bold
look through the mists to horizons of gold.

A Wish For a Friend

Blessings be yours – and all felicity.
Come shine or shadow, happy may you be . . .
Every good gift may Fortune give to you:
. hope, health and peace – and friendships fond and true.

Time grant to you the harvesting of dreams –
and may your path be lit with golden gleams,
so that you walk down bright and pleasant ways.
Light be your heart and sunny be your days.

Time

Tender and light is the touch of time upon the wound of grief . .
Gentle the pressure of the years that bring the heart relief.

Time from our memories draws the sting – thus we forget the pa
Only the sweetest recollections of the past remain.

Dark turns to dawn and sight to songs, harsh notes to harmony .
Death leads to life and love lives on through all eternity.

Someday Soon

Someday soon, if fate be kind, these lonely days will seem
like a long forgotten story — hazy as a dream.
Someday soon the sun will shine, the shadows all depart,
and the old sweet happiness steal back into the heart.

Someday soon we'll be together, side by side again.
Quickly then we will forget the past with all its pain,
as we face the future years afire with faith and zest,
hoping they will be for us the brightest and the best.

Sweet Is the Dream

Sweet is the dream that comes upon the tides of memory,
like a lovely ship afloat upon a quiet sea.
The dream in which I live again the unforgotten past –
the dream that never fails to come, and seems too sweet to last.

Waking, sleeping, it is there: the dream that has no end:
the thought of you, my dear companion and my heart's true frien
From the evil of the world, its sorrow and distress –
I escape into my dreams, there find happiness.

Thoughts Go Home

Thoughts go home, unbidden – when we're somewhere far away.
Thoughts need no compelling. Off they wander, night or day,
To seek the places and the faces dear unto the heart:
The spot where all our journeys lead, and all roads end and start.

Thoughts go back. They know the way. They need no road or guide
To cross the hills and rivers and the oceans that divide . . .
And though with friends we may abide as round the world we roam,
To the place of heart's desire thoughts turn. Love leads them home.

Music

Music is a language, universal in its scope,
expressing every shade and tone of human fear and hope.
Bliss and grief and all that lies between those two extremes:
sorrow, wonder, exultation and unspoken dreams.

All mankind can know and grasp and understand these things:
the fingers on the keyboard, and the bow upon the strings . . .
Men need no interpreters their message to impart –
when they speak through music in the language of the heart.

When You Hope

When you hope, you turn your face
　　away from sorrow and despair –
and you see the light of heaven
　　that is shining everywhere.

When you hope, you lift a latch;
　　a door swings back and you behold –
broader views and brighter prospects,
　　fair green vistas touched with gold.

Though your heart is sad and troubled,
　　doubt not in the bitter hour . . .
When you hope you prove your faith,
　　acknowledging God's gracious power.

Between the Lines

When we write a letter to a dear one far away,
words fail to express the meanings that we would convey . . .
As the pen moves on the paper recollections start –
a face is pictured in the mind; a voice speaks in the heart.
Though we write of humdrum things and everyday affairs,
behind the words lie all our dreams, our longings and our prayers.
Hopes outpace the written word and thoughts leap on ahead.
And memory between the lines entwines her golden thread.

The Turning Point

There is a milestone on life's path
    that brings us to another start,
where brighter vistas open out,
    where clouds grow light and break apart . . .

There is a spot on every road
    where ruts give place to smooth green ways;
the place that marks a new beginning,
    and the hope of fairer days.

Are you weary of the journey –
    does your burden seem too great?
Are you fighting uphill battles,
    struggling with a hostile Fate?
The milestone at the turning point
    may be a few steps round the bend.
Courage! . . . This may be the spot
    where joys return and troubles end.

The Tapestry of Time

Life works out a pattern on the tapestry of Time.
The threads of hope, of love and grief, of fear and faith sublime,
of happiness and bitterness, of joy and misery,
are stitched into the great design of human destiny.

Within so vast a frame, our tiny patch we cannot see.
Too close we stand to trace the pattern on the tapestry.
But someday, looking from afar, perhaps we shall behold
our little bit of the design; our own small thread of gold.

Yesterdays
and
Tomorrows

Visiting Hours

How much they mean, how sweet they are to those who have
to lie
Week in, week out in hospital and how the minutes fly!
When neighbours, friends or relatives appear beside the bed.
All too quickly comes the time when goodbyes must be said.

They come, they go, and you are left your own thoughts to
pursue
Thinking over all the bits of news they bring to you.
From a life that seems to be a thousand miles away
From the little world in which you live from day to day
Hoping, praying, wondering how long it's going to be
Before you're ready to go home, before you're fit and free.

Underneath the Earth

Under the earth the bulbs lie deep,
Buried in their winter sleep.
Under the frosts the seeds are sealed
In garden bed and furrowed field.
Under a shroud of seeming death
They wait for April's warming breath:
Iris, tulips, crocuses,
Daffodils, anemones.

In the hard unyielding ground,
The sapless roots are locked and bound.
Below the crust of morning time,
Nature dormant bides her time.
Lilac, lily, cherry, may
Await their resurrection day.

Yesterdays and Tomorrows

God of my yesterdays, I have forgotten
All that I failed in when put to the test.
Yet somewhere the whole of my life is recorded
Things unremembered and still unconfessed.
Time buries much and the years fly so fast,
I'll need Thy forgiveness if judged on the past.

God of the future and times not yet planned
All my tomorrows still rest in Thy hand;
The moments, the hours and the days yet to be
Are veiled from my view but are known unto Thee . . .
Thou seest the place where the road will be hard.
Go Thou before me, my Guide and my Guard.

The Vigil

When you watch beside the bed of someone who is ill,
In the dark and silent time when all the house is still,
You keep your vigil hour by hour. The world outside seems
dead.
You pray for strength and cling to hope, although it's just a
thread.

But when the first faint gleam of dawn dispels the night's cold
gloom,
New life comes in with the early light that steals about the
room.
How welcome is the morning as the shadows fade away.
How sweet it is to know God has sent another day.

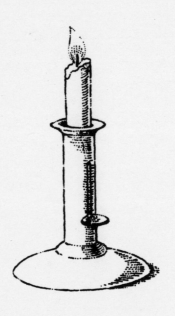

Taking Things Well

You have to learn to take things and to take them humorously.
A blow, a knock, a jibe, a shock, whatever it may be.
You have to take what hits you in the course of every day,
Learning how to take things in a gay, good-natured way.

You have to learn to take some pricks and maybe lots of stings.
You cannot go through life escaping the unpleasant things . . .
Someone's bound to hurt your feelings, but although it's hard,
Never let them see the tears or catch you off your guard.

A Birthday Wish

Down sunlit pathways may you travel all through life, my
friend,
With hope to light your morning way and peace at journey's
end.
Though storms may gather here and there and mists obscure
the view,
May you never fail to find a little patch of blue.

This my wish for you, that you will have the power to see
A bright horizon through the storm-clouds of adversity.
For if you bring a happy heart to each experience,
You will always walk the sunlit paths of Providence.

June Bride

Married in the month of roses when the year is in its prime,
And all Nature is rejoicing in the glow of summertime.
Married in the lovely season when the sun is high and bright,
When the air is sweet and fragrant and the days are long and
                                                              light.

Happy be the bride of June, not only on her wedding day,
But may she have the joy we wish her all the while and all the
                                                              way.
May she cherish in her heart this glad and glorious memory –
To keep the flame of love alight through the years that are to
                                                              be.

The Sunshine House

Make your house a sunshine house and open windows wide.
When the air is fresh and fragrant let it get inside.
Do not shut it out, but let it blow into your room,
Bringing in the sound of songbirds and the scent of bloom.

Even though you live where there's a grey and gloomy view,
You yourself can be a window that the sun gleams through . . .
Make your life a House of Sunshine, cheery, bright and gay:
A life that shines and gives out light to all who pass your way.

The Day We Met

If I could live one day again, one day out of the past,
I'd choose the day that we two met, for when my mind I cast
Across the landscape of the years, it stands out bright and bold.
The memory is evergreen, although the tale is old.

A lovely summer afternoon, a blue and golden sky.
A garden by the water and a white sail moving by . . .
And someone coming up the path I'd never seen before –
Walking straight into my life to stay for evermore.

First Love

First love is a precious thing that comes when all the world is
new.
The bloom of Springtime is upon it and the sheen of morning
dew.

First love often ends in heartaches . . . cruel then this life can
seem,
Looked at through the broken windows of a lost and lovely
dream.

When we're young the first sweet passion is a pleasure tinged
with pain . . .
And when it dies, we never think that we shall ever love
again.

Something Happens

We think we've got our lives all figured out.
We face the future sanguine and serene.
We think we know just what it's all about –
Then something happens, something unforeseen.

It doesn't do to plan too carefully.
To be too sure, too clever, or too wise.
For often things work out quite differently.
God takes a hand and springs a big surprise.

Sentiment

Why do we love to keep old letters, hiding them away
In a corner where we keep our dreams of yesterday?
Can it be because we find it hard to make a break
With some recollection kept alive for old times' sake?

Memories are made of unseen threads and silken strands,
Yet they bind us closely like the grip of iron bands.
Fondly do we treasure as the changing years advance
Letters that recall the days of youth and of romance.

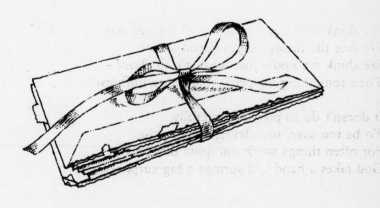

Wonderful Day

If you're looking for things to be awkward about then you
won't have to look very far.
A hundred excuses for making complaints you can find on the
spot where you are.
Life hands you a grievance as soon as you rise, if your thoughts
take that natural line.
There'll always be something to start you off grumbling if you
are determined to whine.

Don't let it happen. As soon as you wake, get your mind in the
right sort of frame.
Whatever comes up take it well, take it gaily. It's all in the luck
of the game.
Look for the best and the good things in life and you'll find in a
strange sort of way,
They come to the one who can greet every morning expecting a
wonderful day.

Twenty-first

It's hard to think of something fresh to say
When somebody is twenty-one today.
It's all been said before so many times
With all the old familiar worn-out rhymes.

And so it's just the same old thing once more.
I wish you health and lots of luck in store.
May Time be kind and Life be good to you.
I hope you'll reach your goal – and dreams come true.
But most of all I hope that you will find
The secret of a wise and happy mind.
For what's the use of money or success
Without the precious pearl of happiness?

Far Away

Far away – by distance reckoned – yet how near you seem to
me!
Separated, yet together in the realms of Memory.

Far away, but here in thought. The miles between us melt
away . . .
Parted, yet in spirit meeting – every hour of every day.

Best Points

Look out for the best points in others,
Look out for the finest things first . . .
Be sure that you've found all the good traits
Before recognising the worst.

Too often, put out by some quarrel
Past kindness we're apt to forget
The ties of affection are severed
By words that we live to regret.

And many a friendship is broken,
Because when it comes to the test
We see only what are the worst points
And fail to remember the best.

Moss

Along the garden path between the worn and crumbling stone,
There are strips of velvet where the soft green moss has grown.

And here and there upon Life's path a broken stone appears.
Yet time is kind – and in the crazy paving of the years,
It covers up the ugly cracks and hides them from our sight,
With the moss of sweet remembrance, ever green and bright.

The Faithful Heart

Faithful to the promise given, now and through the days to be.
Bound by ties of fond affection – and the cords of memory.
Absence proves the heart's devotion – testing Love's
                                                    sincerity . . .
Steadfast in a world of chaos – shines the star of constancy.

Never

Never give up hoping. There's nothing to be lost.
Never give up trying, however great the cost.
Never give up climbing, though clouds obscure the view.
Never give up striving, your purpose to pursue.

Never give up trusting the hand of Providence
To lead and guide you safely through every circumstance.
Never give up praying whatever else you do.
Never give up saying that all is well with you.
This is faith dynamic, the power most wonderful,
The faith that moves the mountain and works the miracle.

Hope Deferred

Do not be despondent when your hopes have been deferred,
And it seems your prayers have gone unheeded or unheard.
Do not be discouraged when your wish has not come true.
Never lose your faith. Be patient. Take the longer view.

Give God time. It's not for you to say just when and where
You want a thing to happen, for the answer to a prayer
Must sometimes be delayed because the Providential schemes
Are wider than the expectations of your dearest dreams.
So learn to wait and learn to trust and never cease to pray.
Often do we find there was a blessing in delay.

Traffic

Traffic is people. Traffic's more than fumes and wheels and
noise.
Traffic is women, men and children. Traffic is girls and boys.
People who are dear to someone. Life is sweet to all.
So take no risk and never let your highest standards fall.

Be courteous to others and consideration show
To those with whom you share the road; with care and caution
go,
Remembering your obligations when you ride or drive.
Traffic is people, like yourself, who want to stay alive.

Let There Be Light

Where there is ignorance – let there be knowledge.
Where hearts are blind and hard, let there be sight.
Where there is falsity – let truth be uttered.
Where evil casts its gloom let there be light.

Exercising the Will

Exercise your will each day to keep it firm and strong
So that you can make decisions, sifting right from wrong . . .
If you do not work your will-power it will atrophy.
Like a limb that's never used, quite useless it will be.

Be Assured

When you give in to despair, you doubt God in your soul.
But remember He is God, and He is in control.
Do you think He has forgotten all your secret prayers?
Be assured He knows it all. He loves you and He cares.

To Your Highest Self Be True

Did you fail to reap good crops when came life's harvest-tide?
Have you failed to reach the mark? And have you been denied
The fulfilment of your dreams? It may seem so to you –
But you have not failed if to yourself you have been true.

Thirsting By the Well

Life's a hard and dusty road, but here and there along the way
There are wells of living water, so that in the heat of day
Man can quench his thirst for God . . . and yet how often we
pass by
Heedless of the green oases underneath the brazen sky.

The Swing

Swing high,
Swing low,
Up to the top of the tree you go,
Seeing the mill at the water's edge,
Seeing for miles over field and hedge.

Swing high,
Swing low,
Down to the ground and then up you go.
Catching a glimpse of the old green pond,
The church in the lane and the woods beyond.

Swing high,
Swing low,
Just like a bird on the wing you go.
But what would you say if the swing swung high,
And left you up there in the bright blue sky?

Pamela Jane

Pamela Jane was caught in the rain,
When walking one Sunday in Sparepenny Lane.
She didn't know whether to hurry and run
Or stand under shelter and wait for the sun.

She found a dry spot where the trees made a roof,
But soon even that was not quite waterproof.
The leaves dropped big splashes that fell pit-a-pat
Right on the top of her very best hat.

Crash went the thunder and down came the hail.
But I've forgotten the end of the tale.
So we must leave her out there in the rain.
Oh what a pity! Poor Pamela Jane.

Mother and Son

I used to take you in my arms and kiss your tears away.
When you were hurt you ran to me. But that was yesterday –
Then you were a little boy and all my very own.
Now you are a man and you must learn to stand alone.

Sometimes when I see that there are troubles on your mind,
I long to bear your burdens and I wish that I could find
A way to show my love for you. But what help can I be?
The years have passed and you have grown beyond your need
                                                    of me.

Lazy Days

If you're on your feet all day with little time to sit,
Have a lazy holiday and make a rest of it . . .
Don't go rushing here and there, but take things easily,
In some quiet country place or down beside the sea.

Many tonics can be bought, but fresh air is the best.
Take a course of Nature's treatment, have a lovely rest.
Then when you are back again inside life's busy maze,
You will feel the benefit of all those lazy days.

Perhaps

If a record could be made
Of every wedding, to be played
In times of crisis and of stress
To recall past happiness,
Perhaps more marriages would be
Rescued from calamity.

Once again unhappy pairs
Could hear the pledges and the prayers;
The sacred vows they made that day –
To love, to honour and obey.

The Lodestar

You are the lodestar of my life. Your love is like the guiding
                                                            light
That brings the mariner to harbour through the darkness of the
                                                            night.
The great ships set their course for home, and on that constant
                                                        star rely
Led by the eternal lamp that burns upon the northern sky.

You are the dream I have pursued across the oceans of the
                                                        years.
You are my hope and my salvation. Yours is the love that
                                            calms all fears.
You are my star of fate and fortune, steadfast, unfailing,
                                            changeless, true.
Safely I'm brought to quiet havens when in my heart I turn to
                                                        you.

Something to Give

We all have something to give the world – and nobody else but
you
Can perform the task that it was destined you should do.
So never feel that you are just a unit in a crowd.
You are an individual with special gifts endowed.

It may be just the gift of spreading cheerful thoughts about –
Or keeping calm when there's a fuss and smoothing troubles
out . . .
We all have parts to play no matter where or how we live.
We all have something to offer life. We all have something to
give.

Moods

April keeps us guessing with her sunshine and her showers.
In the wake of storms she brings the rainbow and the flowers.
First she smiles a radiant smile and then she frowns and broods.
It is hard to keep up with her ever-changing moods.

Do not be like April, one day bright, the next in tears,
Always at the mercy of your moods, your hopes and fears . . .
Live life in the sunshine of a gay philosophy
One that does not vary with the winds of destiny.

Pleasures Unsought

The loveliest song I ever heard
Came from the throat of a tiny bird,
When a torrent of lark notes pure and high
Poured through the quiet of the downland sky.

The loveliest picture I ever saw
Was something no artist could paint or draw –
When the moon trailed a streamer of silver light
Over the sea on a summer's night.

The loveliest things it seems to me,
When looking back in memory,
Are those that we do not seek or find
By an effort of the mind:
The beauty glimpsed, the music caught.
The pleasures that come to us unsought.

Let It Pass and Let It Go

Do not hang on to a grievance. Let it pass and let it go.
Do not cling to hurts and grudges. Life is very short, you
know.
Bear no malice, never harbour thoughts of bitterness or spite –
Whether you are in the wrong or whether you are in the right.
You can't afford to let the poison seep right down into your
mind.
Try to think of something else and very quickly you will find
The trouble loses its importance and in time will fade away.
So if something riles and rankles turn it out without delay.

You must take the generous view however much you've been
upset.
You've got to let the grievance go. You've got to drop it and
forget.
If you're hard and unforgiving in the things you do and say
How much mercy can *you* hope for on the final judgment day?

The Blessings of the Years

Do not count the passing years, but count your friends instead,
Remembering the old friends and the new.
Do not count the milestones as the road of life you tread –
But the good things God has given you.

Don't add up the birthdays as they come and as they go –
With vain regrets that Time flies all too fast . . .
Count the happy memories that set your heart aglow;
The blessings of the present and the past.

Here at the Gate

I want a new dream, a new hope, a new heart.
I'd like to be able to make a fresh start –
With nothing to worry or weigh on my mind –
Mistakes all forgiven, the past left behind.

Here at the gate where a new year begins,
I wish I could shed all my sorrows and sins,
But Life's not like that. Though you tread a new track,
The old load you still have to bear on your back.

You can't drop that burden. It's still yours to bear,
But this you can do; you can start with a prayer –
Not to be given an easier load
But a new vision to light the old road.

Resolution

I will do what life demands, whatever it may be –
I will work with willing hands, and conscientiously
Strive to put the best I know into the task I do.
With God's help I will be faithful, steadfast, just and true.

Communion

Busy I shall be this day, but I must vow to take
A quiet moment here and there, a secret prayer to make.
Moments of communion we need from hour to hour
To draw from God the things we need: hope, courage, grace
and power.

Eyes to See

Behind the turmoil of the world with all its clamourings,
May we always strive to hear the rush of angel wings . . .
Behind the common scenes of life, though drab they seem to be,
Shines the glory of the Lord for all with eyes to see.

Stronger Shoes

Do not ask for smoother pathways, but for stronger shoes to
                                                        wear,
So that you can climb the mountains, and a heavy burden
                                                        bear . . .
Do not wish for easy times, but for a greater courage pray –
So that you can meet with joy whatever comes with every day.

The Silent Garden

Silent now the garden lies
Under dark and stormy skies.
Days are short and nights are long,
Frosts are sharp and winds are strong . . .
One by one the petals fall
From the last rose on the wall.
Winter's breath is in the air;
Birds are mute and boughs are bare.

Yet no bitter tear we shed,
For we know they are not dead.
We, with faith unquestioning,
Say there'll be another Spring.
At the end of Winter's reign,
In the garden once again,
There'll be blossom on the spray.
None can take this hope away.

Why then should our faith sink low,
When some loved one has to go
Out into the great unknown –
Out into the dark alone?
Death the victor may appear.
But remember, year by year,
New sap rises in the tree.
Life goes on eternally.

My Quest

Thy truth I seek – no other quest is worth the toil and agony.
Thy love I seek – no other love can satisfy me utterly.
Thy joy I seek – Thy joy is life, is hope and health and energy.
Thyself I seek – for Thou art God and every good exists in
Thee.

Resurrection

Round the dark and troubled world the bells of Easter ring,
Bringing to our weary hearts the message of the Spring.
Season of awakening, renewal and rebirth,
Mystic resurrection of the glory of the earth.

Hope revives and joy returns and faith is now reborn
In the light that cometh with the resurrection morn . . .
As we hail the risen Christ His image we can see,
Shining through the loveliness of field and flower and tree.

Pledge of immortality in every living thing,
Promise of eternal life in seed and leaf and wing . . .
Love has triumphed over Death. The stone is rolled away.
God has granted unto us another Easter Day.

Nature's Wonderland

For all our vaunted cleverness we cannot understand
The beauty and the mystery of Nature's wonderland.
The sun, the moon, the whirling stars, the sea, the sky, the
earth –
All the many miracles of life and death and birth.

Man with marvellous machines can do stupendous things
But could not with his hands create a bird with voice and
wings.
Could not make a rose, a rainbow, or a common weed,
A chrysalis, a dragonfly, a cabbage or a seed.

Cannot say what magic holds the planet in its place
Or how the spider spins its dainty web of fairy lace . . .
He cannot make a blade of grass, a leaf, a cone, a pod
Yet he is too arrogant to give the praise to God.

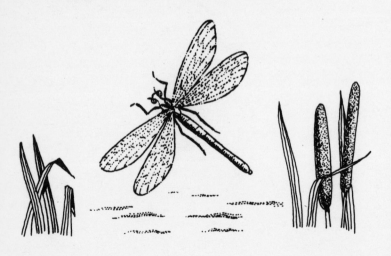

Tomorrow

Do not let your faith be shaken by the touch of sorrow,
But remember God is good and there will be tomorrow . . .
All must strive and suffer – that's the way it has to be.
Life's a skein of twisted threads: joy, laughter, tragedy.

Never doubt. Hold on and hope though hope seems all in vain.
Sooner than you think perhaps the sun will shine again . . .
Troubles and misfortunes come to put you to the test,
Proving strength or weakness, bringing out the worst and best.

No one wants to weep with you if you are always sad.
Lonely you will never be if you are brave and glad . . .
Search the clouds – you're bound to find a gleam of light to
                                                    follow
Though today is grim and grey . . . remember there's
                                              tomorrow.

Baby's Hand

There are many lovely things: stars, rainbows, birds and trees,
Roses, mountains, butterflies, the skies, the earth, the seas,
Petals, dewdrops, cones and berries, seeds and shells and sand –
But nothing half so lovely as a baby's little hand.

Just a scrap of dimpled flesh, a tiny, tender thing,
Softer than the silken feathers on a linnet's wing,
Thumb and fingers, veins and nails, a perfect work of art.
Weak, and yet it has the power to move the hardest heart.

Many busy hands we'll need our better world to build –
If the hopes for which we've suffered are to be fulfilled.
So when you see a baby's hand take hold of it and pray –
That God will use it for His work somehow, somewhere,
                                                someday.

Wedding Rings

Engagement rings may vary as to price and size and kind –
Diamonds, sapphires, pearls and rubies, many types you find,
But wedding rings all look alike in platinum or gold.
No matter what they cost to buy, or whether new or old,
They all look very much the same upon a woman's hand –
Plain and unpretentious, just a little simple band.
Yet every one is different, for every one you see
Has a story of its own, a secret history.
The tiny hoop, although so small, holds all the world for two,
Enclosing them within the circle of a dream come true.

He Planted a Tree

He planted a tree in memory of his beloved wife.
When she went, it seemed that there was nothing left in life.
Nothing but the dear remembrance of the days gone by:
The happy days before Death came to break Love's golden tie.

But year by year, the tree he planted grows before his eyes,
And every springtime, when the new leaves open to the skies,
It seems to bring a promise of the life that is to be.
And his heart draws comfort from the Tree of Memory.

The Acrobat

I love to watch the bluetit with his promise-tinted front –
Turning crazy somersaults. It's like a circus stunt . . .
Upside down he hangs and pecks a juicy bit of fat.
No mistake about it, he's a first-class acrobat.

Watch him with the monkey nuts. He has the greatest fun.
He swings and clings and picks the precious nuts out one by
one.
Agile as a star performer on a high trapeze,
He jerks and jiggles, twists and wriggles with the utmost ease.
And when a bit of coconut is hung out on the tree,
With his claws he gets a grip and nibbles skilfully.
It's as if he sets out to amuse and entertain.
I do believe he knows we're watching at the windowpane.

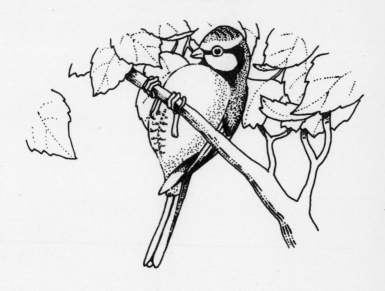

Prayer

Prayer changes funk into courage. Prayer changes night into day.
Prayer changes gloom into glory and pushes the mountains away.
Prayer changes everything somehow in ways that we can't understand.
Prayer makes us wiser and stronger to cope with life's daily demand.

Prayer is the link that connects us with God in His heaven above.
Prayer brings us into the presence of Him who is power, life and love.

Regrets

There's always something to regret, however much you've
                                              done
To help to make life happier for a beloved one.
However deep your grief may be, thoughts come to trouble you
When there's no more you can say and nothing you can do.

You recall misunderstandings; trivialities
Steal out of the past to spoil the sweetest memories,
Things that haunt the house of sorrow, things you can't forget.
So lose no chance to prove your love. Have nothing to regret.

Doubts

Doubts breed in the shadows when the lamp of Faith burns
low.
Doubts creep up out of the darkness and in strength they grow,
Crawling from the secret places, thriving in the gloom.
One by one they take possession of the inner room.

Once the glow of Faith is dimmed, the doubts will multiply
Until there is no corner left for Hope to occupy.
So keep alight the lamp of Faith, for in its steady beam
Doubts will vanish like the phantoms of an evil dream.

Have a Heart

Have a heart that tries to feel what other people feel.
Have a heart – a sympathetic word will often heal
The hurt of one who stoops beneath a weight that none will
                                                    share,
With nobody to lend a hand and nobody to care.

The world is full of people needing all that you can give.
Old folks feeling lonely with a few brief years to live.
Children badly treated, all around you everywhere
Are sufferers with trials to face and crosses they must bear.
They need your love. They need your strength, they need your
                                                kindly hands.
So have a heart, a heart that feels – a heart that understands.

Learning to Live

It's a hard and a difficult business, this business of learning to
                                                                live,
Knowing how best to make use of the knowledge that the
                                                passing years give.
To muster the technique of living is something not learnt in a
                                                                day,
For only experience teaches and time alone shows us the way.

It's an art to be studied and practised, to achieve a degree of
                                                            success.
It's a ding-dong of trial and error: some succeed – others never
                                                            progress.
It takes time to discover the right way of coping with people
                                                        and things,
And it's not until life is half over that we learn how to take
                                                    what it brings.

Magic

There's a magic about the sea: it casts its own strange spells
On the lonely shores among the rocks and pools and shells.
By harbours where the fishermen spread out their nets to dry,
And at the gay resorts with all the traffic roaring by.

There's a fascination watching waves by day and night
Curling softly on the sand or breaking foamy white.
On windy cliff or crowded beach, by quiet cave or quay,
It's there; the ancient magic of the everlasting sea.

My Friends

Fate has often led my footsteps to a place of destiny,
Where I found a kindred spirit, someone waiting there for me.

For all other precious things I've searched and struggled,
                                    worked and fought,
But my friends, the best and dearest, these have come to me
                                    unsought.

A Sense of Humour

If you see the funny side, you'll stroll along the sunny side
While other folk are walking in the shade.
Things will never harass you, embitter or embarrass you.
A sense of humour is the finest aid
To wisdom and philosophy. In trouble and adversity
It brings you smiling through the stress and strife.
So cultivate the power to see – the little touch of comedy
Behind the trials and tragedies of life.

A Seat in the Sun

It's known in the town as the Grandfathers' Seat,
And on days that are sunny and fair
The same little group of old folks can be seen,
Sitting enjoying the air.
Smoking and joking and nodding a bit,
Watching the crowds hurry on.
Sifting old memories, thinking long thoughts.
Talking of times that are gone.
God grant all grandfathers joy and content
And peace when their life's work is done.
For what could be better than this at the end?
A pipe . . . and a seat in the sun.

It Helps

It helps to talk things over if you're anxious or afraid
When hurt or worried, and there are decisions to be made,
Problems though gigantic tend to dwindle when discussed.
It helps to open up your heart to someone you can trust.

Someone sympathetic who will listen and advise.
Someone who will share your trouble – someone kind and wise.
When there's a tangle to untie and life makes hard demands
It helps to talk it over with a friend who understands.

Roses Everywhere

Here again comes lovely June! No place on earth can show
Such beauty as our Britain in the summer's early glow.
Washed by softly falling rains the grass grows greener here
And where else on this globe does Heaven seem to be so near?

Carpeted with buttercups the golden meadows blaze.
Wild flowers flow along the verges of the country ways.
Bright is every cottage garden in the winding lanes
With jasmine and with honeysuckle at the windowpanes.
Gardens bright with candy-tuft, with thrift and irises.
Pathways edged with lupins, pansies, pinks and peonies.
Stocks in rainbow tinges that cast their sweetness on the air.
And roses white, pink, gold and crimson. Roses everywhere.

The Best

The best is never over, there is always something new,
Another start, another chance, another road for you.
Another mountain top to climb though hopeless it may seem.
A fresh adventure beckoning, another dream to dream.

The best is never buried with the ashes of the past.
The best is where you look for it. No happiness can last
But other joys are granted if you press on faithfully,
Believing in the promises that 'the best is yet to be'.

Time Is Life

You can't buy or borrow a minute. Time isn't for sale. Time is
                                                          Life.
Yet how we squander and waste it – in worry and folly and
                                                          strife
And things of no value or merit – the pleasures that die with the
                                                          day.
If Time were for sale how we'd treasure the hours that we
                                                   fritter away!

Spend Time as you spend gold or silver. Spend wisely what
                                            Time God may give.
Time wasted is Time gone forever. It can't be recalled to relive.
And when at the last Time grows precious and Time is the
                                          thing that you lack
You think of lost friends and lost chances and the days that will
                                          never come back.

Life Is Now

You can't put life aside, for life is now. Life is today.
Life is not tomorrow and you cannot turn away
From problems and experiences that you have never sought,
Just because you're unprepared for what the day has brought.

You've got to deal with every moment as it comes along
Making your decisions wise or foolish, right or wrong.
Life won't wait until you've got things sorted out somehow.
You've got to live it, ready or unready. Life is now.

On the Way

Here come snowdrops once again; they look so small and frail,
Yet how sturdily they stand against the wintry gale.
Set on stalks of tender green, they swing their fairy bells,
Grouped about the gates of Lent, like ghostly sentinels.

Once the snowdrops have arrived, a change they seem to bring.
The days begin to lengthen and the birds begin to sing.
The earth may still be frosted and the skies be wild and grey,
But the snowdrops whisper that the Spring is on the way.

The Happy Life

All men seek the happy life; down many roads they fare,
Searching for a pleasant path away from strife and care,
Looking for some hidden turning where the sunlight gleams,
Following their star of fortune down the track of dreams.

Restless, never satisfied, life's winding ways they wend,
Always thinking there'll be something better round the bend –
Pressing on towards some distant castle in the blue,
Never pausing where they stand, the present scene to view.

Learn to live each passing day as if it were the last:
Do not dwell in thought upon the future or the past.
It is good to dream a dream; it helps you on your way –
But remember you can live the happy life . . . Today.

A Foothold

Home is a foothold in the world, a spot that we can make our
own.
Who'd want to be a wanderer, a restless soul, a rolling stone?
The world is big; too big for me. I have no wish to rove or
roam.
Give me four walls, I care not where, and I will make myself a
home.

Sunward

Keep on looking sunward although the skies are grey.
Keep on looking forward towards a brighter day . . .
Clouds may frown above you, but always keep an eye
On the golden edges that gild the stormy sky.

Keep your thoughts turned sunward and dwell on happy things.
Let your hopes rise upward like birds on soaring wings.
Face the right direction until the sun appears.
Turn towards the brightness, away from doubts and fears.

Green Fingers

Some have green fingers . . . their gardens will thrive.
In every weather their plants will survive.
Soil may be poor and the air may be cold,
Yet 'neath green fingers – bulbs shoot and unfold,
Defying the foes that attack other flowers,
Seeming to grow by miraculous powers . . .
Blight cannot touch them and pests cannot harm,
Held in the spell of some magical charm.

What is the reason? Does anyone know
Why one will die and the other will grow?
Flowers have their feelings. Yes, Flowers understand –
If there is love in the touch of a hand.

Dark Cupboards

I have planted my bulbs in their bright coloured bowls,
And I've put them away in the gloom
Of a little dark cupboard; it's hard to believe
That they'll live in the darkness, and bloom
In a glory of purple, of white and of pink,
From those small thread-like roots in the mould.
I shall watch the great miracle under my eyes
As the close-clustered petals unfold.
There are dark little cupboards in everyone's life
Where we hide all our secrets away –
Griefs, grudges and fears and frustrated desires
Thrust aside from the light of the day.
Could we open our cupboards and bring them all out
Of the darkness – perhaps we should find
The green tips of friendship – fresh flowers of new hope
Growing out of the depths of the mind.

The Tempter

When hope sinks low and courage fails and everything seems
                                                    wrong,
That's the fatal moment when the devil comes along,
Tempting you to doubt God's goodness and your faith deny –
That's when you must be on guard, the tempter to defy.

He's always there, the trouble-maker, looking for a chance
To weaken you, to trip you up and hinder your advance.
He's always near you, whispering and plucking at your sleeve.
So when tempted to give in, stand fast, hold on – believe.

Courtesy

It smooths the path and oils the wheels, a little courtesy.
It sweetens our relationships. How different life would be,
If everyone would be polite, considerate and kind.
It would help to ease the hardships of the daily grind.

It doesn't cost us anything, and yet it means so much;
The tone of affability, the sympathetic touch;
The civil word, the charming manner; geniality –
Showing unto friend and stranger simple courtesy.

Fairy Castles

Planning for the future, and dreaming golden dreams!
That's what keeps us going; a foolish thing it seems,
But all men have their longings and treasure silently
Their own idea of Heaven, and happy days to be.

It is these secret visions that keep our hopes awake.
Without something to live for the heart would surely break.
It speeds the laggard moments and helps us struggle through –
To plan our fairy castles and build them in the blue.

Sewing

In and out the needle goes along the folded seam,
While your heart is following some lost and lovely dream.
In between the stitches you can go a long, long way,
When you're sitting sewing at the quiet end of day.

O, the things that you remember as you draw the thread!
Odds and ends of memory come back into your head.
Names and faces, times and places, round the world you go.
Many miles you travel as you watch the stitches grow.

The Great Thought

Lean upon the thought of God, a great thought let it be,
Large enough and deep enough to rest in, utterly.
Finding consolation, hope, refreshment and release
In the quiet comfort of His presence and His peace.

Lean on this, for this alone will take your whole full weight.
And will make you strong to face whatever be your fate.
Every other staff and stay will be of no avail.
Lean upon the word of God for this will never fail.

The Lamp

The Word of God is like a lamp. It shines upon the unknown
                                                      way –
And sends into the darkest place, a steady glow, a guiding ray.
Light Eternal burning ever as towards the Truth men grope –
Leading them by hidden ways along the paths of faith and
                                                      hope.

While You're Waiting

While you're waiting for tomorrow, get the best out of today.
While you're waiting for the sunshine don't complain at skies of
grey.
While you wait for future pleasures don't forget the ones you've
had.
Call to mind the things enjoyed, the happy times and not the
sad.

While you're waiting for the granting of the wish you hold most
dear,
Don't lose sight of all the joys that life can offer now and here.
Times of waiting can be fruitful and to you much good can
bring.
Make the winter yield a blessing while you're waiting for the
Spring.

Dividends

Make Life pay dividends. You can if you choose,
For it's a business. You gain or you lose.
Though you have problems and troubles to meet –
Don't accept failure and loss and defeat.

Profit by everything. Wrest good from ill.
Double your assets of wisdom and skill.
Turn to advantage whatever Fate sends.
Increase your happiness. Add to your friends.

Showing the World

If you've a song,
Try it.
If you've a tear,
Dry it.
If you've a cross,
Bear it.
If you've a joy,
Share it.
When Hope grows faint,
Brace it.
When trouble comes,
Face it.

Where there's a wrong,
Right it.
When life is grim,
Fight it.
If you've a hand,
Give it,
If you've a creed,
Live it.
If you've a faith,
Show it.
And let the world
Know it.

Dreamer

Dreaming of the things you mean to do some other day.
Always dreaming of tomorrow, wishing Time away.
Dreaming of the happiness that is eluding you.
Never doing anything to make the dream come true.

Dreaming of the lovely things you think you want or need.
Dreaming of the roses, never working at the weed.
Dreaming of a goal but never shouldering a load –
And really setting out to face the hazards of the road.

Dreaming of a harvest when you never touch a plough.
Dreaming of the future and forgetting Life is NOW.

Colouring

Colours make the beauty of the earth and of the sky.
Grass-green meadows, clay-brown land and white clouds
floating by.
Golden dawns and rosy sunsets and the lovely tones –
Of colourings in gems and jewels, shells and rocks and stones.

Garden flowers and country flowers in varied rainbow hues:
Pinks and purples, grey and silver, lavenders and blues . . .
What are colours? How would you define them to the blind,
So that they imagining, could see them in the mind?
Yellow corn and wine-dark rose, a butterfly's bright wing.
How could you explain in words this thing called colouring?

Seeing

The eyes are wonderful indeed, for with them you can see
Big things like a sun, a moon, a mountain or a tree –
And little things like glow-worms, seeds and dewdrops
                                        diamond-bright.
Marvellous beyond all telling is the gift of sight.

You see a vision of the world as through a pane of glass –
And those outside can see your thoughts as through the mind
                                        they pass;
Anger, sorrow, joy: the greatest brain could not devise –
So clever a contrivance as the windows of the eyes.

Looking at Life

Don't condemn the world because you don't like what you see:
Trouble and unhappiness, greed, vice and misery . . .
Certainly these things exist and cannot be denied –
But don't forget that there is something on the other side:
Courage and unselfishness and much that's good and kind.
It really all depends upon the focus of your mind.

Don't let dark distorting shadows spoil the world for you.
The fault may lie within yourself, so change your point of
view.
Instead of looking on the bad and dwelling on the worst –
Try to get a broader vision, putting best things first . . .
Turn the camera round: a different angle strike.
You will get another picture – maybe one you'll like.

Aspect

If you build a house, consider aspect first of all.
Do not let the sunbeams play upon a solid wall . . .
Plan your windows so that every room with light is blessed –
Catching all the brightness as the sun moves east to west.

Thoughts like windows must be made to face the brightest
way.
Set them in the right direction when you plan your day.
Providence may smile on you or fortune seem unkind.
So much will depend upon the aspect of your mind.

Turn yourself away from things that anger and depress.
Do not live behind a wall of grief or bitterness.
Break it with a window that will open up a view.
Face the way the sun is shining. Let the light get through.

Let There Be Peace

Keep the peace within your soul, unmoved and unafraid.
Face the worst that life can do, by nothing be dismayed.
Build an inner sanctuary of secret happiness –
Rise above your daily worries, fretful thoughts suppress.

Try to make an inner world of faith and quietude –
A temple of tranquillity where strength can be renewed –
Where joy can grow and hope unfold and confidence increase.
Outside may be conflict . . . but within let there be peace.

When Sorrows Come

We wonder why it has to be when sorrow comes our way –
The horizons of the morrow turn from gold to grey . . .
All the lovely things we dreamed of vanish overnight –
Looking out along the road we see no gleam of light.

Where then can we look for hope to break the dark despair –
When the cross of our affliction seems too hard to bear?
Where then can we turn for consolation and relief?
Where find balm to ease the heart and heal the wound of grief?

Only in the knowledge that all things are transient.
Nothing in this changing world is fixed or permanent.
It is but the shadow of the great reality –
A place of preparation for the life that is to be.

To a Colleague on Retirement

We're sorry you are leaving us. We'll miss you every day
But all must reach this turning point upon life's winding way.
The time has come to leave the desk at which you've worked
                                                    and won
The warm affection and the real respect of everyone.

So congratulations! May the future bring to you
Many blessings, many friends, and life begin anew . . .
We wish you health and happiness and all prosperity.
Your task here may be finished, but 'the best is yet to be'.

The Joy of Gardens

In a fair and fragrant garden God created Man.
It must have been His wish for us, His purpose and His plan –
That we should learn to love the trees, the birds, the grass, the
flowers.
The story of the race begins in Eden's pleasant bowers.

The love of gardens still remains a joy that never dies
For the poor man and the rich; the simple and the wise . . .
Whether it be planted in a wide or narrow space
He who makes a garden makes the world a sweeter place.

The Mystery of Prayer

We know not what we do when for our absent ones we pray.
We know not how the magic works – but somewhere far away
Someone receives a blessing, and is comforted
Silently around their path the angel wings are spread.

Though from them we are divided. Love will bridge the gap.
We know not what strange powers we touch, what secret
                                        springs we tap
When we kneel and earnestly commit them to God's care.
Great things are accomplished through the mystery of prayer.

Green Is My Garden

Green is my garden and gay are the flowers.
Lovely the trees in the sun and the showers.
But what can I do with these midsummer hours,
Without you?

Red are the roses that bloom on the wall.
Sweet is the music when morning birds call.
But there is a sigh at the heart of it all –
Without you.

A Glimpse of England

Water-meadows rich and green where herds of cattle graze.
An old stone bridge round which there clings a dream of
bygone days . . .
Streams where pollard willows stoop and graceful swans glide
by.
Pools that hold the lights and shadows of the changing sky.

Across the fields the Minster towers rise up as if to crown
The quaint old streets and houses of the little market town.
This is what we fought for! For this we shall hold fast.
The beauty that is England – and the glory of the Past.

Look Forward

Look forward and your hopes will rise.
Look forward!
Though stormy clouds frown in the skies.
Look forward!
The steps of Time you can't retrace
Press onward at an eager pace
Towards some finer, fairer place –
Look forward!

Look forward with a hopeful mind.
Look forward!
Resolve to leave the past behind.
Look forward!
You can't afford to let your gaze
Turn back to rest on other days.
Down brighter, better, broader ways
Look forward!

Safe Keeping

I pray for your safe keeping with every hour that chimes
Through all the pain and peril and terror of the times . . .
My thoughts are ever with you although we are apart –
In daytime and in darkness, you're in my mind and heart.

We cannot be together these troubled hours to share.
But may you be protected. This is my constant prayer.
Though dark the days of danger and dire the storm and strain.
God have you in His keeping until we meet again.

Wild Forget-me-nots

When bees hum in the linden tree and roses bloom in cottage
plots
Along the brookside banks we see the blue of wild forget-me-
nots.

Shy flowers that shun the prying eye – content to let the daisy
hold,
The glances of the passers-by – with brazen stare of white and
gold.

Forget-me-not! From long ago it stirs the thought of happier
days
For memories like wild flowers grow – along the heart's
untrodden ways.

Judgments

Don't judge with haste your fellow men – see only what is true.
Ignore the worst, bring out the best, and take the charitable
view.
I hope God does the same for us, and sees the virtues, not the
vice.
If He remembered only faults – who'd ever get to Paradise?

Thoughts Go Home

Thoughts go home unbidden when we're somewhere far away.
Thoughts need no compelling, off they wander night or day
To see the places and the faces dear unto the heart —
The spot where all our journeys end, and all roads end and
start.

Thoughts go back, they know the way. They need no goad or
guide
To cross the hills and rivers or the oceans that divide.
And though with friends we may abide, wherever we may
roam
To the place of heart's desire thoughts turn . . . love leads them
home.

The Sun Is Old

The sun is old, as old as Time, but every dawn is new.
The light of all created life has burned in heaven's blue
Since that first sweet daybreak when the sun sent down its rays
On a green and sinless world of fresh untrodden ways.

The sun is old, beyond the span of mortal reckoning
Yet every golden sunrise is a new and glorious thing.
Every time the morning glory lights your windowpane –
It can be a new beginning. Life can start again.

The Shallows and the Deeps

Quiet and shallow are the waters where the leafy willows
sway.
Yet this little winding river flowing gently on its way
Is going out to meet the sea and swell the ocean's rolling tide.
The stream will widen to embrace the mighty waves where
great ships ride.

Uneventful life may seem, a narrow stream of nights and days
Yet somewhere in the future it will open into broader ways.
Every soul in God's own time is called unto its destiny –
To steer its course alone upon the waters of Eternity.

The Magic
of
Memories

OLD MOTHER
NATURE

The whole web of life is held together by unseen threads of relationships between human beings and animals, but the most marvellous relationship of all is that which binds us to Old Mother Nature.

Spring

Only a God with a thinking Mind could have thought up the joys of Spring—tinting the grass with an emerald dye and teaching the birds to sing—covering hazels with powdery tassels that shimmer in every breeze—spraying the almonds with rosy pink petals and hanging the cherry trees—with bridal-white blossom, and staining the copses with patches of flowers growing wild: celandines, violets, bluebells and primroses, lovely and undefiled.

Only a God with a loving heart could have made us a world like this—where you wake up one morning and find the air as soft and as warm as a kiss—A world where like magic the daffodils come with their trumpets all glowing and bright—as if He repeated the Genesis fiat and said again, Let there be light . . . Blind evolution could not of itself have created a butterfly's wing—Only a God could have ever designed it—so praise Him, the God of the Spring.

Somehow Things Come Right

A mountain loomed before me—too steep for me to scale—and suddenly I saw It: that pathway through the vale—where cliffs of rock rose steeply to block the forward view—but somehow I was guided. Somehow I got through.

A problem like a mountain I saw confronting me: a trouble overwhelming. No hope there seemed to be—of finding a solution. But someone must have prayed—for help to me was given. The right decision made.

It seems that unseen forces are rushed to meet our need. God sends a guardian angel to strengthen and to lead—when stricken in the darkness and lost without a light. I know not how it happens, but somehow things come right.

The Rifts That Make The Glory

*I*t's not until the clouds are broken that you realize—that behind them there was an expanse of golden skies . . . It's the rifts that make the glory. When they break apart—you can see the shining edges where the sunrays start.

Always on the other side of every cloud in view—the sun is waiting glowing in a sky of heavenly blue . . . Here there is a parable for all who can discern. In the clouds there is a lesson for the heart to learn.

Every cloud of disappointment or adversity—hides the sunshine of God's presence—Him we cannot see—behind the stormy clouds that loom like mountains in the sky—but we see the Light Eternal when the clouds pass by.

Make It A Wonderful Day

Whatever the weather with sky black or blue—Whatever the problem that's troubling you—Whatever the prospect, whatever you do—make it a wonderful day . . . How is it done when the clouds draw a blind—over the brightness? It's all in the mind. Make your own glory wherever you go—seeing the sun through the rain and the snow.

When you awake in the morning from sleep—don't let your thoughts slip away and go deep—into old grooves of depression. Take charge. Your willpower assert and your vision enlarge . . . Turn them by force to the right attitude—away from the wrong and the negative mood. You are the master, so they must obey. Make it a wonderful day.

So Good A Land

Where else could you see in such a very tiny space—so much beauty? Tell me, is there any other place—on this overcrowded earth where you with one brief look—could see a bluebell wood, a fairy glade, a rushy brook—and a field of wheat beyond where flowery verges drift—in a haze of clover, daises, columbine and thrift?

Move the eye a fraction and your vision will extend—taking in the view that opens where the meadows end—and you see a cottage deep in clouds of applebloom—underneath a hill ablaze with gorse and yellow broom.

Where else are such pictures set within a frame so small? Only in our little England do the soft rains fall—in gentle showers that bring to life the seeds that make the green. Where else will you find so good a land, so fair a scene?

Winter's Gift

*B*one bare trees against a sullen sky. Fog and frost and wet winds shrieking by. Raw dark mornings and tracks of rutted mire—leading to hayrick, stable, barn and byre.

This is the winter in the country's heart—a grey isolation in a world apart—but this, too, is winter as the long night falls: the flicker of firelight on familiar walls.

There is a healing in the winter's mood. Sated on summer's ripened plenitude—I walk in the quiet fields—and gratefully feed on the gleanings of austerity.

Always New

I thought I knew all about roses—but every time they appear—I see as a bright bud uncloses—a beauty unnoticed last year . . . They never repeat a performance—-No season is ever the same . . . I thought I had seen all the colours, the crimson, the gold and the flame—but here is a rose peeping in at the door. I swear that I never saw this one before.

I thought I knew all about thrushes—but I must admit I was wrong—At dusk or when morning sky flushes—they come with a new kind of song . . . The notes they have practised since Eden—I know them by heart theme by theme—and yet when they sing in my garden—I listen as if in a dream—They sing the old songs with the same measured range—yet something about it is wondrous and strange . . . Bored we become with what science supplies—but Nature is always an endless surprise.

Life Flashes By

Midsummer Day has come and gone. Slowly the sun now loses height. Summer's rich splendour lingers on. Roses still cluster, but day and night—the glory is waning. The peak is passed. Time makes its reckoning all too fast.

Life flashes by as we older grow. Each passing year rushes swifter by. Where do the runaway seasons go? Vainly we wonder and question why—but we can't bid the beautiful moments stay—or call back one hour of a a lovely day.

Gather your memories secretly—so you can dream when you are old—living on Summer's legacy. Even though life turns grey and cold—you will never feel lonely, lost or sad—recalling the happy times you had.

Spring Was Yesterday

*I*t was only yesterday that I looked out to see—blackbirds nesting in the hedge and blossom on the tree—daffodils and hyacinths—and now the creepers glow—rose and crimson on the wall. Where did the Summer go?

In a flash it came and went. I tried to hold it back—by counting every moment, but it passed and in its track—Autumn weaves a leafy carpet, russet, flame and red—where the golden goblets of the crocuses were spread.

Why does time increase its pace? It should be otherwise. Every year should be longer but each one swifter flies . . . Summers used to linger, now they hurry on their way. Looking back it seems to me that Spring was yesterday.

Rose In The Rain

*R*ose at the window pressed close to the pane—lifting your face to the tears of the rain—over the hill, reaching up from the spray—Joy you have brought to an invalid's day.

Seen through the sheen of the silvery shower, keeping me company hour after hour—bright in the lightning that splinters the sky—poised on your stem with the wind blowing by.

Rose at the window—I've watched from my bed—and lovely you looked with the storm overhead—What is the magic? The secret explain—How to hold on till the sun comes again.

Younger You Would Like To Grow

Younger you would like to grow, but even if you could—Would you really wish to go right back to babyhood? Wouldn't it be awful if you had to face the years—dwindling back to childhood with its tantrums and its tears.

Growing old we all regret, but it is better far—than getting younger day by day, things being what they are . . . Wisely did the good Lord plan that we like swelling grain—should grow towards maturity and growing older gain—the wisdom and the understanding that the years can bring—if we go on looking forward, learning, ripening.

Every day add something to the treasury of Time—so that when you get beyond the zenith of your prime—you don't go back, but onward and you welcome every stage—richer, stronger, wiser for the garnerings of age.

A Change of Mood

*T*here's a wintry touch in the air today, a fleck of frost on the holly spray—and more than a whispered hint of death in the smell that comes on the wind's rough breath: the smell of leaves that decaying lie—under the grey and grieving sky.

But a change of season need only be—a change of rhythm, a change of key—a different mood and another phrase—in the symphony of the passing days . . . Summer and Autumntide, Winter, Spring. Each has it's own good gift to bring . . . Enjoy then the year with it's changing themes—thankful because there are no extremes.

Travel the world and you'll never find—a climate where Nature is half so kind . . . Gently we pass from the Autumn's glow—to the Winters that bring but a little snow: a few brief weeks when the birds are dumb—when the long nights drag and the sharp frosts come—but even when April seems far away—God often sends us a beautiful day.

Bubbles In The Sky

*H*ow lovely are the clouds of March—under heaven's spreading arch! Foamy chariots riding by—across the highways of the sky . . . Upward we look surprised to see—so huge a mass move suddenly—like a thousand flags unfurled—above the mountains of the world.

And when a driving wind prevails—they resemble billowing sails—dipping across the waves of space—as if competing in a race . . . Feather-light the big clouds break—Bursting like bubbles they froth and flake—floating off into the blue—beyond the measure of our view.

The Holidays

*T*rain the children not to waste the precious holiday hours—Teach them how to think and look at berries, leaves and flowers—Educate the little ones to study Nature's ways—Open a new and wonderful world for them in holidays.

Freed from the schoolroom let them wander, wondering at it all—Let them see the glorious splendour of a waterfall—Draw their active minds away from mere mechanical toys—discovering the magic of strange things and deeper joys.

Of richly-painted butterflies and graceful birds in flight—of sun and shadow breaking through the curtain of the light—Woods where great trees lean above a softly singing brook—Feed them with the knowledge to be found in Nature's book.

The Bend By The Signpost

We've turned the bend by the signpost that bears the word to Spring—We've come a few steps nearer to the moment that will bring—the hallelujah choruses to garden, wood and lane—telling us that life is stirring in the soil again.

We've turned our backs on Winter though still the winds blow cold—we see beneath the budding tree a flash of fairy gold. Daffodils and crocuses are massing out of sight—preparing for the festival of colour, life and light. This is the month of miracles, the season of rebirth—when beauty breaks the seals and springs triumphant from the earth.

THE MAGIC
OF MEMORIES

*Human beings are inventive, some even
clever, but no-one has ever been clever
enough to explain the workings of memory.
Nor has anyone been able to tell you what a
memory is, where it comes from and where
it goes when it has passed through the
mind. Memories are our invisible
companions.*

Make Me A Memory

Make me a memory—something to treasure—after the glow and the glamour have gone . . . like some old melody—bringing back pleasure, strangely and tenderly lingering on.

Say something wonderful—words I'll remember—if Time in passing should tear us apart . . . Life takes its course. Love must burn to its ember. Say just one thing I can hold in my heart.

Give me a day of delight and perfection—with never a shadow, or pang of regret—a day to recall with a loving affection—to cherish for ever and never forget.

Only Another Milestone

Do not count the passing birthdays with a tearful sigh—Let them come and let them go as Time goes flying by—Never waste a moment on the things that you regret—If you've sought forgiveness—say Amen—and then forget.

Thank God that another year now lies ahead of you—for living and for loving—Take the optimistic view—Every day with grateful heart expect a miracle—looking out for something that is good and beautiful.

Travel hopefully along. Don't say the best has gone—Birthdays are the milestones but the road goes winding on.

Beautiful Moments

I opened wide the window to the morning of the day—and from the wintry branches of the trees across the way—I heard the robins and the thrushes fluting joyously—and it seemed that they were singing specially for me.

I stood and listened. Every note was like a silver bell—and deep inside my heart I knew: I knew that all was well. A word of hope had reached me through the birds . . . I can't explain—But that lovely message had not come to me in vain. A thrill of new expectant life along my nerves had run—as, looking up, I felt the warm sweet kisses of the sun.

One Perfect Day

*D*id you ever live one perfect day—When everything you did or said or thought—was in the spirit of the One who brought—the light of life to guide us on our way? Did you ever feel when night brought rest—and your heavy lids began to close—that in every matter that arose—you had practised what you had professed?

No. You never did, for are not we—fallible and human? None is good. We know so much, yet have not understood—the simple truth Christ preached in Galilee . . . We fail, as all must fail unless they pray—for strength of will to keep the soul alive. Tomorrow, while there's time, resolve to strive—To conquer self—and live one perfect day.

The Harbour Of Contentment

*O*ff to my treasure isle of dreams I sailed on the morning tide—with only my hopes for compasses and only my star to guide . . . Seeking for happiness I called at many a far strange port—then on I sailed unsatisfied, for I knew not what I sought.

Over the oceans of the years I travelled but never found—the lost horizon; so sick at heart I turned my ship around—towards the place I had started from. To that haven of rest I went—home on the flow of the evening tide to the harbour of content—There to discover what I had wandered round the world to find. It was there all the time awaiting me: contentment and peace of mind.

The Key Word

Do you think that happiness resides in just what you possess? Seek that happiness within—and every morning will begin—with thoughts of joy and gratitude—Cultivate the attitude—that life is sweet and life is good—if God's great laws are understood.

Do not say you cannot see—the glimpses of divinity—behind the drab and commonplace—you feel the everlasting grace—but only with your inner sight—can you perceive this hidden light: this aura, making dull things shine—with splendour from a source benign

In the crowds that throng the street—a radiant face you seldom meet—so marked they are with lines of care. A sunny countenance is rare . . . The world with all its sham and show—can't tell you what you long to know: the key word that will heal and bless . . . The secret of true happiness.

Confession

Lord, I cannot see the way. So hour by hour and day by day—let me place my hand in Thine—lest I miss some vital sign—a turning to the left or right. Lord walk with me and be my sight.

Lord, I often fail to hear—Thy guiding voice although so near—for quiet is the tender word—the loving message scarcely heard—above the strident clamourings of urgent claims and wordly things.

Lord, this life is hard to live. My many weaknesses forgive—and in Thy mercy see my need. Without Thee I am lost indeed.

Power Of Happiness

When the mind is happy the heart is happy too. Picking up the message, the body takes its cue—and the feet, responding, walk with lighter tread—as thoughts like merry dancers go whirling round your head.

Brightness, like the sunshine, sparkles in your eyes. Somehow you feel better as your spirits rise . . . Hope and health together blend in harmony—Nervous tensions slacken, calmly, quietly.

Cheerfulness works wonders. Gaiety can be—potent as a tonic. Nature's remedy—for the ills and ailments that weaken and depress. Simple but effective; the power of happiness.

Somebody's Tomorrow

*I*s anyone the happier for meeting you today? Has anyone been prayed for just because he came your way? Has anyone been helped because you stopped to lend a hand—spared a little time to listen, tried to understand?

Has anyone been made to feel that God was somewhere near? Has someone somewhere been relieved of worry and of fear? . . . Has someone rediscovered faith in what is good and true—seen another side to life, another point of view?

If the answer's Yes, then you have earned your night's repose. If No, your day was wasted, spent in vain—and at its close—there can be no satisfaction; not unless you say—that somebody's tomorrow will be better than today.

Beyond The Easter Mystery

At the time of daffodils—when Spring across the windy hills—comes a-dancing wild and gay—there comes this dark and solemn day, the day when God was crucified—and as a common felon died—to rise again mysteriously—the risen living Lord to be.

O miracle most marvellous that God could come and suffer thus! To reappear and reassure his friends, that they too could endure—what lay ahead; for He could see beyond the Easter mystery—when He, the Christ would come again—in glory and with power to reign.

The Uncompleted Tapestry

*A*fter a bereavement when the last word has been spoken—the tapestry is laid aside. The thread of life is broken—the growing pattern that evolved out of the worst and best—can never be completed now. Unfinished it must rest . . . The hand that held the needle can no longer draw the strand—but somewhere on the other side a new design is planned.

And you, now left alone, must take the skein of mingled hues, the crimsons and the violets, the scarlets and the blues—and start to work upon the uncompleted tapestry—Not the same, but different, and lovely it could be—with glowing tints of memory to give a bright relief—like threads of fire embroidered on the canvas of your grief.

The Quiet Ways

Walk slowly when you walk in lanes for there is much to see—the russet bracken on the banks, the structure of a tree—when autumn winds have stripped it naked, bare against the sky. You'll never know what you have missed, if rushed, you hurry by.

Tread softly when you enter churches. This is holy ground. A mind attuned to quietness can catch the muffled sound—of all the prayers and all the praises that have risen here. Voices echo in the silence for the listening ear.

Go gently as you go along the noisy ways of life. Move graciously amongst the crowds, the turmoil and the strife . . . Speak lovingly to children, to the stranger and the friend. Speak kindly. Never with your tongue your fellow man offend.

Old is Beautiful

A church or a cathedral, brick and stone—
stained by Time in every mellow tone—of gold,
moss-green and grey. The hallowed walls—seem
to be alive when sunlight falls—on altar, lectern,
windowpane and pew—with a sense of peace
surrounding you . . . Old is beautiful.

A face—where there is written line by line—
the manuscript of life; the open sign—displaying
what the changing years have wrought—Eyes
where joy lights up each passing thought. Hands
grown frail with work done willingly—in the
service of Love's ministry . . . Old is beautiful.

When I Said Goodbye To You

I said goodbye to the Summer when I said goodbye to you—I said goodbye to the roses, to the sea and the downland view—It was a wonderful Summer, but all the time I knew—It could not last forever. No dream like that comes true.

And so we floated together, as on a tide of dreams—A brief but strange encounter, incredible it seems—viewed from across the river of everyday concerns—A little candle of happiness was lighted and still burns—in the hidden cavern of that secret place—where I keep the memories that time can never efface.

It's All In The Logbook

It's all in the logbook: the ports of call, the daily incidents—the warnings, the weather, the calms, the storms, the hour-to-hour events . . . The maritime journal must be completed be it dark or light—the readings of compasses, charts and stars—all there in black and white.

And every soul is a kind of ship as the sea of life it sails—every detail of what occurs in sunshine or in gales—is all in the logbook; good deeds and bad. The truth you cannot hide—when the Pilot takes you into harbour on the evening tide.

The Way I Used To Take

*T*his is the way I used to take –Up through the woods that fringed the lake—Over the hill and into the lane—Down to the village then home again . . . Past the old church with its Saxon well, its Norman font and its English bell—Under the bridge where the kingfishers flew—at the river's edge where the cowslips grew.

This is the way I used to take—Never foreseeing that man would make—a hell of my heaven: an ugly place—devoid of beauty and of grace . . . Lacking in character, naught left to feed—the heart in its spiritual need. House by house identical. Every one with its aerial. Is this the way I used to take—or am I dreaming wide awake?

Three Eyes

*I*nsight, foresight, hindsight. We have within the mind—the power of looking inwardly, and forward and behind—wonderfully are we made. This is a mystery—how in separate directions we can look . . . and see.

No-how can we understand the workings of the brain—how thoughts can switch from off the track, can go and come again—Delving down into ourselves then flashing suddenly—forward to the future and then back via memory.

TAKE A LITTLE TIME

Take a little time for seeing—grass and blooms with dew impearled—Take a little time for being—Quiet in your own small world . . . Take a little time for sowing— flowers amongst life's many weeds— Someday you will see them glowing— growing from the hidden seeds.

Take a little time to ponder—what is in your secret heart—Take a little time to wander—in the silence set apart . . . Take a little time for living—busy though your day may be—Take a little time for giving— happiness to somebody.

The House of Remembering

How could I not remember you—when at every turn—you move amongst the shadows where the lamps of memory burn? Something of you lingers still around the home we made—for happiness paints its pictures in tints that never fade.

Sometimes I catch an echoing, so soft that I scarcely hear. I open a door and seem to feel you intimately near—No sadness marks your coming and going. In every room you leave—a joy beyond the power of telling. Why then should I grieve?

Friends say this house is haunted—why not look for somewhere new—but how could I bear to go? Here I belong because of you . . . Here then I shall stay as one by one the years slip on—for in some other place perhaps I'd find that you had gone.

The Greatest Gift

Give your child a good foundation in the things that matter—then when come the shocks and disappointments they won't shatter—their faith in life; if kicked around on solid ground they'll fall—knowing there's a God above who is the judge of all.

You can give your child no greater treasure than The Book—in which the laws of life are written. Make them learn and look—and find the secret blessing that mere money cannot buy. With this they'll have the power to fight, all evil to defy.

Do not satisfy their cry for every trivial thing— give them words of wisdom and your precious gift will bring—something that will give a beauty to the fresh young face—the refinement of the touch of spiritual grace: a light to banish doubts and fears—and lead them safely through the years.

Where Day Meets Night

I walk in my garden in the evening hours—for this is the moment to commune with flowers. The dusk drops its curtain and it seems to me— they too are conscious of a mystery—For when they are smiling in the sun's full glare—of me and my presence they are unaware—sharing their secrets with the singing birds—lost in an ecstasy that knows no words.

But when I seek them and the hour is late— they meet my mood and we are intimate . . . I touch them lovingly though veiled from sight— in that strange borderland where day meets night.

Let Love Speak

Let the word of peace be spoken—when relationships are broken. Let Love speak and heal the smart—of wounds inflicted on the heart.

Let Love's language, sweet and tender—its own gentle service render—saying what is kind and wise—with the lips or with the eyes.

Let no grievance leave an ember—that perhaps you may remember—and regret in later years—with your penitential tears.

Try forgiving. Try confessing. Let Love speak the final blessing—casting every doubt away—before the closing of the day.

What Might Have Been

*T*hink of me a little as the busy days go by. Never quite forget what might have been . . . In between the crowded hours make room for memories—evoking from the past some lovely scene—a recollection from the void—of the thing we have destroyed.

For everyone there's somebody, but sometimes things go wrong—Confusion follows, and the wires get crossed . . . Foolishly mistakes are made—discordant notes creep in—and one day you discover love is lost.

My Memories

Lord, what do you ask of me, a big or little thing? Whatever it might be, I will obey . . . Take the treasure of my heart though close to it I cling—but never take my memories away . . . because they are the unseen threads that hold me to the past—without them I should lose identity . . . Deep into a grey and timeless world I should be cast—and looking back, no milestones I should see.

So be it Lord, take what you will of what I now possess. Whatever be demanded I will pay: sight or hearing, health and strength, life's greatest happiness—but never take my memories away.

Feeling Hurt

*H*owever hurt you're feeling—hide the secret scar—Time will bring its healing. See things as they are.

Try to be forgiving—loving more, not less. Life is meant for living and for happiness . . . Maybe someone somewhere is feeling sorry too—longing for the whisper of a word from you.

Time To Go

*T*he last rose lingers on into December—clinging to the skirts of old November—Like a ballerina ageing fast—who wants to go on dancing to the last.

Sad, but proud, unwilling to surrender—dreaming of the heyday of her splendour . . . Tears of rain from off her petals flow—as the cold wind whispers, "Time to go".

Lose Yourself In Other People's Troubles

Lose yourself in other people's troubles—by lending them a sympathetic ear—for troubles lost perhaps will be forgotten—and in the end will even disappear.

Lose yourself in what is all around you. The whole wide world outside your door is there—with neighbours, colleagues, relatives and strangers—who too have crosses difficult to bear.

So if you're feeling lonely or despondent—just treading up and down the same old ways—go take a look at other people's problems—and lose yourself in someone else's maze.

The Puzzle

A sparkle of light on the floor I could see—A bead or the stone from a brooch it could be—I stooped to retrieve it, but nothing was there. My fingers outreaching clutched only the air . . .

It was a sunbeam entrapped in a ray—that somehow from millions of miles far away—had come from the big burning ball of the sun—where its long journey to earth had begun.

Foolish to snatch at this flicker of light—Trying to capture a jewel in flight. How came the sunbeam to fall on my mat? Useless to ask such a question as that. Why pose a puzzle none can expound—tapping at doors where no answer is found?

Learning To Count

When folks complain you sometimes wonder if they ever had—the sort of education that would teach them how to add . . . You do not have to get degrees life's problems to surmount—All you have to do is stir your memory and count . . . your blessings day by day . . . If you can't see them you must be—mentally blind or deaf, for all around your eyes should see—evidence of things you took for granted through the years—So instead of boring people with your trials and tears—Reach for pad and pencil and each day write out a list—of mercies granted, blessings sent—and let not one be missed.

Teaching The Children

*T*here's time to eat, but seldom time to think—Time to wash the dishes in the sink—but seldom time to spare or time to give—in teaching the little ones how best to live—How to speak and how to train the mind—the pearls of truth and wisdom there to find.

Try not to miss the opportunity—to lift the veil upon the mystery—of life itself and what it's all about—Teach them the Way, dispelling every doubt—Protect them and direct them to the Man—who died to give the world a master plan.

THE HAPPY PEOPLE

Who are the happy people? The people who are free—from self and its dictation, the people who can be—quiet and unoffended when hurt or brushed aside—not concerned with saving their faces or their pride . . . These are the happy people. They never have to fight—to express a grievance or maintain a right.

The unassuming people of little wordly worth. What did the Master promise? He promised them the earth! The gentle-hearted people who don't ask much of life— are rich in all that matters. Content, avoiding strife . . . Never provoking trouble or stirring enmity. These are the happy people for they are truly free.

Something Happens When You Smile

When you come to think of it a smile's a funny thing. Give it and you get it back, and often it will bring—happiness to somebody you never even knew: neighbours, fellow-travellers or strangers in the queue.

Lift the corners of your lips and in the glass you'll see—a transformation and a change of personality . . . Eyes can smile as well as lips. They catch your mood and glow—even though your heart be breaking and your spirits low.

Practise at the mirror when a moment you can spare. Try. You'll be surprised to see the face reflected there . . . Somehow you seem brighter and you feel that life's worthwhile. Isn't it amazing? Something happens when you smile.

A Year Is Born

We wish each other happiness as every new year chimes. And we want it for ourselves, good days and happy times—but do we make too much of it and is there too much stress—laid on the importance of this thing called happiness?

A happy and a bright new year; the customary phrase! Happiness is sweet . . . but in these grim and troubled days—May it be a useful year, a year of work well done; a busy year of goals attained and moral battles won.

It's a strange and holy moment when from belfry towers—the clocks strike out the solemn message of the midnight hours. A year is born . . . O pray for wisdom as it comes to birth—to do your share and build God's kingdom here upon the earth.

Harmony

Let us work for Harmony in every walk of life; harmony instead of discord, jealousy and strife; if we live in harmony, no jarring note destroys peace of mind—relationships, and all our precious joys.

Harmony of voices. Let no ugly sound be heard—bickering or bitterness, the shrill and angry word; may the voices in the house be soothing and refined; quiet and happy, saying only what is good and kind.

Harmony throughout the world. Oh, may we live to see—Christ's own Kingdom. Not a dream, but a Reality. Every nation in the world united, and yet free—working out their destinies in perfect harmony.

Between The Acts

*T*here are intervals in life. The show can't run non-stop. In between the acts there comes a pause. The curtains drop. Circumstances take a hand and something unforeseen—comes along and breaks the pattern of the old routine. Illnesses, upheavals or a cruel turn of fate—call a halt and there is nothing you can do but wait.

While you're waiting learn the grace of faith and fortitude—as your life is being changed and problems are reviewed—Intervals there have to be; accept them. Face the facts. Wisely use the quiet times that come between the acts.

Coming Or Going

Do not say you're going through a time of suffering. Say you're coming through it. That's a very different thing. Coming through your trouble to the brightness round the bend. Coming through the tunnel to the sunshine at the end.

Coming through with banners flying, stronger every day. Coming through, not going through—with Hope to lead the way . . . Coming through your difficulties. Coming through your test—coming through the worst and yet believing in the best . . . No matter what life does to you—Always say you're coming through.

What Shall I Give?

What shall I give? You ask each year as Christmas days draw nigh. What can I do for those I love—what present can I buy? What shall I give my feelings to express and to convey—for the festival of love we keep on Christmas Day?

What shall I give? said God, unto my children there below—struggling in the dark. What gift of joy can I bestow? . . . I will go myself, He said, as one of them to be. I will visit my creation. They My face shall see.

This will I do to prove my love and teach them how to live. More I cannot do for them and more I cannot give. I Myself will be the gift within a human frame. I will give them Christmas to remind them that I came.

Your Blessings

*T*hough you may be passing through a dark and anxious time, smile and keep your courage, for surrender is a crime. Gratitude works magic, like the waving of a wand. Lift your eyes above the shadows to the world beyond.

With a glad and grateful heart, you'll take a different view. Think of all the benefits that fate has showered on you. Do not dwell upon misfortunes and the tears you've shed; count your blessings, drop your cares, and count your joys instead.

So when in the morning you awake to greet the day, do this little sum before you go upon your way. Add up all your blessings, past and present, great and small; you will find that Life is not so empty, after all.

You'd Be Surprised

You're never as ill as you think you are so do not be dismayed—if your mirror tells you you are looking old and frayed. It's only a passing phase. You'll soon be feeling fit and fine. Tomorrow or the next day you will sparkle. Eyes will shine . . . It's wonderful how a hopeful thought can change your point of view—so that courage, health and strength come flowing back to you.

You're never as wronged as you think you are when something you resent—and never as hurt as you say when putting up an argument . . . You'd be surprised how rapidly a grievance fades away—if you can think of something else and drop it for today.

How Did It Happen?

*V*iolets by the woodland way. Promise of blossom on the spray. Wonderful glow of daffodils—underneath the windowsills—and by the verges of the lane—primroses beaded with the rain.

Glorious splash of crocus gold—as in the sun the cups unfold. Thrusting of tips where frosts still cling. Wonder of hyacinths opening. Fragrance of daphne on the breeze. Beautiful pink of almond trees. Just as if somebody overnight—had cast a spell and lit a light—by some act of wizardry. How did it happen? You tell me.

Be Your Own Best Friend

Be your own best friend. A friend—and not an enemy—so that if you're left alone you're in good company—Learn to love the silences that steal in here and there—as you sit and think your thoughts before an empty chair.

Know yourself and teach yourself contentedly to live—independent of the world and what it has to give . . . Train your mind to gather gold from every passing day—so that you will never have to wish the hours away.

Come to terms and to yourself a good companion be—one to be relied upon when life is out of key . . . Loneliness you'll never know and peace you will possess—if you have within yourself the root of happiness.

Not The Answer

*P*arting is not the answer . . . That way lies defeat—disaster and disruption, failure and retreat—The way together forward is the way that we must take—Resolved to face the future, side by side, without a break . . . Making something good of life and something that will last—To our wedding vows remaining true and holding fast—Not parting, but starting all over again, beginning now today—Parting is not the answer. Let us try the other way.

THE TONE
OF A HOME

One can have an intimate relationship with a home whether it be a cottage or a mansion, a flat in a busy town or a house in a suburb. A home consists of four walls. First it is formed by the impersonal hands of the builder, next it becomes the property of the people who live, sleep, eat and think in it and it is what is thought, said and done within these walls that determines the atmosphere of a home. Take care. Restrain tempers and tongues. Harbour no grievances. Let the music of kind words be the daily theme around which the tone of the home is built up and sustained.

Tongues

*S*peak with quiet reverence of spiritual things. Guard the doors of speech against the ugly word that brings—evil in its train. Take not the Lord's dear name in vain. Honour what is good and holy. Shun what is profane.

Tongues can bless and tongues can curse. Much power do tongues possess—making trouble, causing strife or bringing happiness . . . Language can be blasphemous, crude, vile and horrible—or it can be pacifying, pure and beautiful . . . Watch your tongue and let no child hear words of violence—and of Him who heareth all—speak well. Give no offence.

Happy Families

Make your home the centre of a happy family—bringing all your friends into the cosy company—where an open door is kept for all to share the fun—Dad and mother always there to care for everyone.

Grandpa, grandma, parents, children. Each has much to give—age and youth together working out the way to live—with mutual respect and lots of laughter to be heard. In such a home you seldom hear a cross or unkind word—Even if you're not all living at the same address—keep in touch inside the circle of the happiness—kindled in the gaiety—of a happy family.

Someone Built A Cottage

Someone built a cottage three hundred years ago—to stand against the weather, the wind, the rain, the snow. He set it stout and sturdy upon a Sussex hill. His work was good to look at and it is lovely still . . . Upon a frame of timber the russet tiles were laid. That roof is still a fine one for it was truly made. The oak of posts and lintels hold every brick secure. Behind their screen of roses the weathered walls endure.

The beams that span the ceiling, so cosy, snug and low—reflect the shine and shadow from sun and firelight glow. The hearth that warmed his children on cold and wintry days—still gives content and comfort within its cheery blaze . . . Someone built a cottage. His name I do not know—but when he made that cottage three hundred years ago—He would have been astonished to know that it would be—a well-loved home for someone in the twentieth century.

Cheerfulness

Cheerfulness is like a lamp that radiates a light—scattering depressing thoughts and putting fears to flight—generating happiness wherever felt or heard—with an optimistic viewpoint or a cheery word.

Cheerfulness can animate the spirit of a crowd. Something happens as when sun comes breaking through a cloud . . . Some there are who have this power to be a medium—that the joy of life flows through whenever troubles come—changing situations when the atmosphere is tense—knowing how to strike the note of hope and confidence.

Grace At Table

*E*very meal is a sacrament. All bread is holy bread—because it comes from God by whom the hungry world is fed—but we, defiant of His laws, upset the balanced plan—destroying what the Lord created for the needs of man.

With fruit and wine, with corn and fish and with the flesh of beast—He prepares before our eyes a rich and goodly feast . . . When you eat remember this. Give thanks and grateful be—to Him who conjures banquets out of river, soil and sea.

Love Is . . .

Love is more than passing pleasures. Love is happiness—found in home and homely treasures that the years will bless . . . Love is caring—Love is bearing—one another's crosses. Love is sharing everything, the profits and the losses.

Love is more than bells and laughter on a wedding day. Love is facing what comes after—sunny skies or grey . . . Love is giving. Love is living just for one another—working out the daily problems of your lives—Together.

This Thing Will Pass

*T*he wind is beating at the pane—in frantic gusts of sleeting rain—Like lashes of a whip it falls on the windows and the walls, thrashing through the tortured trees—at the house, while I at ease—sit in comfort safe and warm—from the fury of the storm.

The demon wind must spend its force—have its hour and take its course . . . Remember this when trials increase. Rest in faith and be at peace. Through the turmoil and the din—Hear that still small voice within—speak above the crashing brass—saying, "Trust. This thing will pass."

Take What Comes

*D*on't expect perfection for you'll never find it here. This is earth, not heaven, so with charity and cheer—take what comes, the good, the bad, and don't start whimpering—when you're disappointed with a person or a thing.

Do not worship idols and complain when you have found—feet of clay beneath the robes in which you've wrapped them round . . . Everyone is human. Do not be too critical—when someone fails. Remember that you, too, are fallible.

Keep your ideals in your heart and set your standard high—but don't lose faith when things go wrong. Just let the storm blow by . . . Do not ask too much of life or reach beyond your range. Accept and learn to live content with what you cannot change.

Silently

Silently the seed swells in the earth—and the unborn child awaits its birth . . . Silently the snow falls, feather-light. Silently the stars dance through the night . . . Silently as in a lovely dream—glides the swan upon the moving stream. Silently roots spread and buds unclose. Silently dawn comes and sunset glows.

Silently the mystic meditates. Silently he watches and he waits. Silently the grail of truth is sought—in the quiet sanctuary of thought . . . Man creates the world's cacophony—by speech and motion. God works silently.

Does It Matter?

When all is said and done—Does it matter—if you're in the third or seventh place? If neighbours have some gadgets that you covet—or colleagues streak ahead in life's made race? No, if you have friends who really love you—and strength to bear the cross upon your back—So long as you can rest with conscience easy—at peace with God and man—What can you lack?

When all is said and done—Does it matter—the thing you won't forget and won't forgive . . . ? A grievance nursed can grow beyond controlling. Stop worrying. Step out of it and live.

Make Yourself At Home

Make yourself at home if you are there—
Enjoy the comfort of your garden chair. Relaxing
in the place you love the best—Forget the jobs
and give yourself a rest.

Could you face the effort and the strain—of
packing all those cases once again?—Rushing off
to Paris, Nice or Rome?—Treat yourself and
make yourself at home.

THE COMPANIONSHIP OF TREES

The place occupied in our lives by the company of trees is closely knit into our relationships with Mother Nature. Most of us at some time have known what it was to develop a love-tie with a particular tree. It was the hawthorn you passed every morning as you made your way through the local park. It was the lilac tree in your own back garden which every Spring used to tap on your shoulder with a spray of purple blossom, as if drawing attention to itself in this its "finest hour", or there was that old oak from which you drew new strength when the wind was wild and the winter bleak. These were more than companions, they had become friends, always there to hold out their own gift to meet your special need.

The Space Between

A garden cannot look its best where trees stand thick in gloom—clustered like a crowd of gossips in a dark old room . . . Trees must breathe and look alive if they are to be seen—with shapely limbs upreaching from a foam of leafy green.

Grateful must they feel when someone comes with axe or blade—to cut the strangling growth; with one swift stroke a space is made—to let the sky weave soft blue ribbons round their nakedness—and the sun with golden touches comes to heal and bless.

We, too, in our crowded minds should dare at times to make—a space where God can enter in, the stranglehold to break—of clawing thoughts that tend to choke, to threaten and destroy—the best in life: things that make for light and peace and joy.

In Between The Stones

*I*n between the stones of life there fall the wind-blown seeds—of friendship, love and loyalty, kind words and kindly deeds . . . Often they may hide for years and never form a flower—Then opportunity in passing brings the destined hour.

You never knew you'd meet someday the one you'd call a friend—to whom your heart would open and on whom you could depend—There it lay amongst the sticks, the pebbles and the cones—the seed that flowered beside life's pathway in between the stones.

First Beginnings

Lovely are the first beginnings of the autumntide—whether you wander afoot in woods or through the forests ride—as birch and bracken turn to gold and Nature holds its breath—between the days of maturity and its seeming hour of death.

Look your last on the year now dying. Look and let it go. Spring will bring its resurrection. Believe; it will be so . . . Every tree will bud, and sap will flow in every vein. Though we, like time, must go when called; the tree will live again.

The Garden Of Stillness

*H*ere is a garden of stillness where no winds run to stir—the statuesque solemnity of cypress, yew or fir—The upward sloping edges, thick with beech and birch—preserve within this sanctuary the silence of a church.

Here in this garden of quiet the mind is unaware—of the track that meets the road—a mile or less out there—As if the trees had here ordained that restlessness must cease—so that all who come may find the benison of peace.

What's The Time?

We are all so busy thrusting through the busy day—Seldom do we taste the joy of lingering by the way—to watch a sunset or a cloud, to ponder or to pray—Yet it seems we never lack a moment just to say, what's the time?

It is always time for taking stock—Swiftly fly the minutes round the clock—But when you ask the hour you get a shock—that makes the world around you seem to rock: what's the time?

Never fail your life to rearrange—taking in things beautiful and strange—Spare a second to absorb the view—that draws your thoughts away into the blue—over the hedge beyond the garden gate—Make sure it's not too early or too late. What's the time?

Did You Not See?

*T*he clock of life is fast and overwound. Where do you think you're going? Whither bound? . . . Slow down—ease up. Rest heart and nerves and brain. Foolish traveller, what do you hope to gain?

The world's a lovely place Did you not know? Have you not stood and watched a brooklet flow—under the arches of a willow tree? That white swan gliding by . . . did you not see?

Autumn

The first faint hint of what is yet to be—a pinkish tint upon the cherry tree—The old Virginia creepers turning red around the timbers of the garden shed—Lovely in its dying, yet how beautiful—September's golden leaves: the autumn miracle.

As sure as clocks and calendars—the year when growing old—cloaks the woods in glory— bronze, crimson, amber, gold—The fires of Nature's making, the flames no man can stay: the mighty conflagration that runs from day to day— Like torches blaze the branches in wood and garden bower—September fades but not before it lives its finest hour.

Time, Never Resting

*T*ime, never resting, works on day and night—No-one can hoard it or hinder its flight—working at healing the wounding of grief—doing its work of repair and relief.

Time's gentle touches make well and make whole—the ravage of life in the mind and the soul. Working unceasingly at its own pace—a pace all must follow, no step to retrace . . . But time is the friend of the one who can see—the blessings to come in the time yet to be.

The Tree Of Christmas

Where Autumn's red and golden ways—merge into a wintry haze—There stands, star bright, for all to see: the wonder of the Christmas tree.

The tree that year by year is lit that man may have the joy of it—and rest from turmoil, sin and strife—under the boughs of the Tree of Life: the tree of peace for all spread wide—rooted in love at Christmastide.

WARTIME RELATIONSHIPS

Many a long cherished wartime relationship has lasted a life time. A danger shared is one that can seldom be forgotten for its roots run deep in the soil of everlasting memories.

Such memories are part of our wartime inheritance, sometimes masked in humour, a traditionally British device for disguising anything that might be mistaken for sentimentality.

Ours Is A Tale

Ours is a tale that shall be told by generations yet to be. Ours is a tale of battles fought through valleys of adversity. Ours is a tale of golden deeds and marvels wrought in blood and tears. Ours is a tale that will outlast the epics of a thousand years.

Write it upon the scrolls of glory. Carve it in marble, bronze and stone. This is the measure of our greatness. Let the long saga now be known . . . Lest in the future men should fail to hold these things in memory—and our sons forget the price that Britain paid for liberty.

A Handful Of Earth

*T*he soldier knelt upon the ground and sifted through his hand—a crumbling clod of German earth; a fragment of the land—that had bred the marching hosts who, flushed with pride and hate—had trampled France and stood triumphant at the Channel gate.

A tear fell on the alien dust. A glad and grateful prayer—surged up in his heart as he remembered, kneeling there—English earth; the Oxford lawns; the fens; the Devon loam. Dorset pastures, Kentish orchards, Shakespeare's meadows. Home.

The House Of Peace

We must build the house of peace on broad foundations, strong and sure—if the things we hold most precious are to stand and to endure . . . Not false friendships of old foes, but friendships proven by the years. Born of blood and agony, of sacrifice and toil and tears.

Let us keep in memory the friendships forged in war's red flame; the friendships of the battlefield, and all who fought in freedom's name . . . Let us not forget old comrades when the sounds of warfare cease. Let us build on these foundations when we build the House of Peace.

They Who Died

They have fallen into step with the immortal Dead. They have joined their comrades and are marching on ahead.

Marching to a goal that lies beyond our mortal sight, Marching to the drums of Heaven, out into the light. They who died in Italy and on the desert plains, on convoy routes to Russia, London streets and Norman lanes,

And still they come, an unseen host, to swell the company, of those who perished in the fight by land and air and sea.

In Passing

*H*e fell upon the field of battle as his boy was born, and did not live to see the coming of that happy dawn . . . Through the secret Gates of Death he left this troubled earth—as the new soul entered by the mystery of birth.

Did they come together at the Gates of Life and Death? Just before the wondrous moment of the babe's first breath—Was there an encounter? Did he touch the tiny hand? Did they meet in passing as they crossed the Borderland?

This Be Their Epitaph

*F*rom the clean hands of the young we take the gift supreme: the gift of life and liberty, the right to work and dream . . . We take what they have won for us: a thing above all price. What do we offer in return for that high sacrifice?

They have served their generation—wise beyond their years—Following their Star of faith through mud and blood and tears . . . We shall remember, though once more we learn to live and laugh. They were the saviours of the world . . . This be their epitaph.

Wartime Friendships

As we make our journey down the winding road of War—We cannot linger very long at Friendship's lighted door . . . We lift the latch and cross the threshold, but we cannot stay. We exchange a greeting and we pass upon our way.

Many fellow-travellers along the road we hail—We fall in step, then off we go along another trail . . . with our wartime friends we part—for so it has to be. But their names are written in the book of memory.

The Fairest Sight In All The World

Silver-winged above the earth men travel through the sky. We are told that in the future everyone will fly—But we, who are an island race, must not forget the sea. Ships have made us what we are and shaped our destiny.

Ships!... The magic word evokes the thought of wind and tide—Docks and harbours, blue horizons, oceans deep and wide—Mighty vessels bound for lands romantic and remote. The fairest sight in all the world: a lovely ship afloat.

Under Orders

*I*f every soldier in the field his course of action planned—If none obeyed the orders issued by the high command, no victory could be achieved, for chaos would be rife. So it is with all who fight the battle we call Life.

We are under orders. God's commands we must obey—Taking not the road we'd choose, but His appointed way . . . Life's an endless warfare; evil sleeps not day or night. We'd rather live at peace, but we are ordered to the fight.

FAMILY TIES

*One way or another your life from its
beginning is shaped by the depth or
shallowness of family roots. Even if you
have no children of your own you have ties
through a brother, sister, mother or
grandmother, father or grandfather,
cousins, aunts and uncles. Lonely indeed
must be the soul who can lay no claim to
ties with anyone. A brother in Timbuctoo
or a second cousin who married a South
African at the other end of the world go to
the forming of blood links. Even if these
persons are never or rarely seen, they
verify your claim of belonging to a family.*

Partners

The first dance of all when they danced heart to heart—they knew, they both knew, it was only the start—of something more wonderful than a mere dance—more than a thrill of a passing romance.

They knew without saying that Love, the real thing—had touched them that night with its shimmering wing. No word had been spoken and yet they both knew—that suddenly all sorts of dreams had come true.

It's many a year since the night that they met—but that first dance they will never forget . . . Then boy and girl and now husband and wife—still happy, still dancing, and partners for life.

From The Family

*M*ore than you think we miss you. More than words can tell. We're sending you this message—hoping you'll soon be well . . . Life's not the same without you. The waiting seems so long. So hurry up—Get better—and come back well and strong.

More than you guess you're wanted. More often than you know—our thoughts and prayers are with you—because we love you so . . . Be patient, brave and hopeful. Have faith and you will see—that God will work the wonder. "The best is yet to be".

Christmas Thoughts

*A*ll the world is young on Christmas Day. Our grown-up worries seem to melt away. There is a feeling that we can't explain—for we become like children once again.

The faith of childhood springs in us anew. Our hearts grow lighter, brighter, warmer too. And life takes on a sweet simplicity. God comes so close—not veiled in mystery—But as a child; a small and helpless thing. The baby Christ, the little Saviour-King. This is the thought that breaks down human pride—the tender thought that comes at Christmastide.

To Live For Always In My Heart

Looking back in memory a baby I recall—the centre of our universe, the dearest thing of all. Next I see a toddler, then a child with laughing eyes. Now a girl engaged to marry . . . Goodness how Time flies!

Soon she'll be a bride and I am wanting her to know—I'm happy in her happiness. The children have to go—and make their own homes somewhere else. It can't be otherwise—but on her wedding day when we have kissed and said goodbyes—the little girl of yesterday will stay behind with me—to live for always in my heart: the child of memory.

The Parlour

We talk about the drawing-room, the lounge, the dining-nook. But I prefer the parlour with its prim and formal look. The word suggests a room that has a Sunday atmosphere—a place where switched-on voices cannot jar upon the ear.

A room for conversation and for sewing thoughtfully—where a woman can enjoy a quiet cup of tea . . . A room of charm and character with curtains crisp and bright—flowery covers on the chairs and paintwork shining white.

The modern home is full of gadgets, comfort, luxury. Customs change and fashions alter. So it has to be . . . Old words pass from use, new words take their place somehow—but what a pity no one seems to have a 'parlour' now!

The Bridges Of The Years

*B*irthdays are like bridges that you cross from year to year: bridges on the road of Time. Old landmarks disappear—as you take the unknown path that lies ahead of you. The end of it is hidden, the horizon veiled from view.

There'll be hills to climb. It can't be easy all the way—with roses everywhere you go and sunshine every day—but cross your bridges hopefully, believing in the best. Face with faith whatever comes and truly you'll be blessed.

Hoping Somebody Would Call

Don't let anyone be lonely in your village or your town. Time erects its barriers, so do your best to break them down—before too many days go by, too many months, too many years . . . Risk a snub and make a gesture. Use your eyes and use your ears—to find out who's in need of friendship and a bit of company. It's the duty of a Christian to be kind and neighbourly.

Sometimes someone dies or to a hospital is sent away. Circumstances come to light and then too late you hear them say—We never knew that there was someone living near in such distress— hoping somebody would call to ease the ache of loneliness.

The Eyes Of A Child

Lovely are the eyes of children, angel-pure and starry bright. Happy, guileless, trusting, candid—shining with the inner light of the uncorrupted mind, by wordly wisdom undefiled. Speak no word to cast a shadow on the clear eyes of a child.

With foolish and indecent haste we force the pace of growth and so—too soon they lose that shining look. Too soon they learn, too soon they grow—Too soon comes knowledge of wrongdoing, sex and vice and violence. Let them be children. Cut not short the springtime of their innocence.

You Pass But Once

Once, only once, you pass along this way. So do the good you mean to do each day . . . If it's worthwhile—it's risky to delay. Tomorrow? What may happen? Who can say?

Those well known lines in many a home you see. A little jewel of philosophy . . . "You pass but once". Your opportunity—is now and here, wherever you may be.

We pass but once! How true those words remain! We're all on the move. We call time back in vain . . . Do not let that good intention wane—because you will not pass this way again.

The Homeward Journey

One road winds over the mountains through storm clouds wild and cold—another runs out to the sunset in a glory of crimson and gold . . . Some go by way of green pastures where the healing waters spring—refreshing the soul that has travelled deep valleys of suffering.

Good is the road that leads forward to comfort, contentment and rest—and good is the road of adventure pursuing an unending quest—but there is a point of convergence—where my road meets your road, my friend—for we're all on the same homeward journey, and all roads are one in the end.

Let's Begin

Let's begin—Yes, let's · begin—with the broken threads of our dreams to spin—a shroud to bury the past away—weaving a new dream for today . . . Resolved to make our marriage work—No effort spare, no duty shirk—Forgiving, forgetting the hurtful thing—To life's many problems new wisdom bring.

Remember that wonderful wedding day? Of course, you do. So let us say—No more quarrelling, no more strife—Come to terms with love and life—behaving well through thick and thin—best and worst . . . Come, let's begin.

LEARNING TO WAIT

Some people are so busy picking up burdens that they forget to look at the date on the label. All too often the burden they think they have to bear today turns out to be the one marked "For Tomorrow". Once you catch up with the folk who are over-anxious to overtake tomorrow you will soon find yourself in a crowd. Far too many people are in this kind of a hurry. Beware of forming a relationship with anyone impatiently anticipating trouble. You'll find yourself being carried along against your will. Learn to wait for what you don't really want. Some unwanted burdens disappear before you can pick them up.

Push Back The Horizon

*P*ush back the horizon. Allow no cloud to bar—your passage to the future. Go forward and go far . . . Ignore the flimsy curtain that floats beyond your view. Never allow horizons to halt or hinder you . . . Force them ever backwards into empty space. Fear no deceptive barriers. They're nothing but mist and lace. Tomorrow calls and beckons. Your star is guiding you. Sail on and trust the Captain to take and bring you through.

The Dreamers

Dreamers can't keep up with those who walk the quickest pace—They like to stroll, while others rush to win life's hectic race . . . Folks who push the rest aside, the hustling bustling kind—forge ahead and seem to leave the dreamers far behind.

But the dreamer sees a lot the other fellows miss—He has time to look around—to feel the sun's warm kiss—Time to watch and time to wonder, pausing here and there—Time to pray and time to ponder, time to stand and stare.

Oftentimes the hustlers flag before they reach their goal—having no resources left of body, brain or soul . . . And the dreamer overtakes them, ambling gaily past—Having come the long slow way, he gets there at the last.

Look For The Best

Look for the best and not the worst in everyone you meet—the friend who knocks upon your door, the stranger in the street . . . Look for the beauty not the flaws in every character—the good intention not the bad, the kindness, not the slur.

Close an eye to faults and failings. You have failings too. Pray that God will do the same and not be hard on you—noting your redeeming points, and not remembering every little weakness in the day of reckoning.

That's our only hope of coming through the final test—the hope that we'll be judged not by the worst but by the best . . . If the Lord ignored our virtues, seeing just the vice—Who would ever get beyond the gates of Paradise?

Seek Ye First

Where to find direction in the chaos all around? That's the question. Where can peace and happiness be found? . . . How can one pursue the high and finer things of life—when the world is torn with hatreds, selfishness and strife?

Seek ye first God's Kingdom. Other guests are all in vain—bringing disappointment and frustration in their train—if we have not sought and found the thing beyond all price: the Truth the Master came to teach through love and sacrifice.

Seek ye first this precious pearl—before all other things—Nothing else will satisfy or give the spirit wings—to rise above despair and with a faith triumphant face—the evils and the ills that now beset the human race.

Greet The New

Let the Old Year pass away. Mourn not but greet the New. Turn your eyes in hope and faith towards the distant view . . . Know that you'll be guided safely down the unmapped road—given strength and courage for the bearing of your load.

Do not let the unknown future fill you with dismay. It is in the hands of God—so go upon your way. Trust in Him and have no fear. You do not walk alone. He leads the faithful in the dark and careth for His own.

Leave behind your grievances, your worry and your woe. Drop the extra burden of your grudges . . . Let them go—so that you can travel lighter with a conscience clear—Out into the great adventure of another year.

Voices

The weakling says, "I'm beaten", but the fighter says, "Not I." The shirker says it can't be done, the worker says, "I'll try." . . . The laggard says he's weary and must drop out of the race. The plodder says, "Keep going at a good and steady pace."

The pessimist, when clouds appear, predicts a rainy day. The optimist declares he sees a gold streak in the grey . . . The grumbler says he's sick of life; work, sleep, the dull routine. The poet says, "The stars still shine, birds sing and grass is green."

The cynic says this crazy world is rushing to its doom. The dreamer cries, "I see the peaks of glory through the gloom." . . . The doubter asks, "Where now is God? No sign do we perceive"—and someone at a cross is kneeling, saying, "I believe."

Wayside Glory

*H*e who walks with seeing eyes along a country lane—now beholds the wayside hedges glorified again . . . Garlanded in vernal green, the twigs once black and bare—lift their rosy coronals into the fragrant air.

Buttercups and bittersweet upon the banks in bloom—underneath the shining fountains of the yellow broom . . . Foam of blossom on the thorn and scents upon the breeze. Gold of gorse and flags of fern around the leafing trees.

Cottage gardens, deep in lilac, greet the passer-by—damson, quince and appleblow delighting heart and eye . . . Happy is the wanderer whose feet unhurried stray—down the lanes of England in the lovely month of May.

Worship

*A*ll around us now we see dissension and dismay. This is what the world becomes when men no longer pray. Fear and hunger stalk the earth, suspicion, greed and strife. This is what the modern creeds have made of human life.

Walk again the quiet ways of faith and charity. Worship Him Who made the earth, the sun, the stars, the sea—God the Father and Creator, Love supreme, sublime—Lord of life and death, of men and angels, space and time.

Let us then to God's own House return with prayer and praise—asking Him to guide us through the dark and troubled days . . . To restore the broken nations and the whole world bless—leading us along the paths of peace and righteousness.

Something In The Heart

*T*here is something in the heart that keeps us strong and sane—in the hour of peril, of temptation and of pain—Bids us cling to life in spite of sorrow and of loss—pointing to the light behind the shadow of the cross.

There is something in the soul that yearns to spread its wings—with the wild desire to breathe the breath of higher things—something that abhors all evil, ugliness and strife—and responds to truth and goodness, beauty, love and life.

Underneath the outward show of personality—lies the holy part of us that lives eternally—This spiritual consciousness that no man can define—that changes human nature with a touch of the divine.

Tomorrow's Burden

Don't pick up Tomorrow's burden while it's still Today. Hour by hour we're given strength our part in life to play—Light sufficient to illume the path that we must tread—Not enough to pierce the darkness of the miles ahead . . .

We in some mysterious way are helped when things go wrong—Shoulders stoop beneath the strain—and yet we get along—finding that we have the power to meet each fresh demand—if we reach out in the dark and hold the unseen Hand.

Never look for storms approaching when the skies you scan. Don't anticipate the future; it's not ours to plan. Do not strain your eyes to see the turnings in the road. Why take on before you must another extra load?

Don't go searching down the byways for the things you fear. There's no need to fight the next day's battle till you hear—the summons of the trumpet and the beating of the drums. Don't pick up Tomorrow's burden till Tomorrow comes.

A Change Of Heart

Yesterday's steps you can't retrace—by slowing down or quickening pace—changing course, or turning back—You still will be on the same old track—The only change worthwhile you'll find—will be a change of heart and mind—leading and directing you—on towards that lovely view.

Keep to the rules and bear your load—along the rough and rutted road—on that wayside seat awhile—gathering strength for the second mile—Keeping an eye on the distant height—that draws you on by day and night—walking tall and walking straight—the better world to recreate.

Upside Down

Upside down and inside out this mad world seems today—When you come to think of it you know not what to say—Are we crazy rushing on along the road to doom—never caring where we're going, never making room—for sober thoughts that lead away from never-ending strife—towards the pastures of a more enlightened mode of life.

Did no-one ever warn us and has no-one ever heard—the voice that in the silence speaks the Everlasting Word?—Blind and deaf and ignorant, this voice we failed to heed—pathetic now we stand unguarded in our hour of need—clutching at a reed to keep afloat and keep alive—the Bible to restore, to resurrect and to revive.

Never Say No

Never say No to Hope, when Hope comes knocking at the door—to bid you look ahead, towards the happier days in store—Never say No to Hope when Hope comes dancing down your way—with something great to communicate, and something good to say.

Never refuse to listen, for she brings a word for you—bidding you take the upward slope that commands the broadest view—But Hope is always in a hurry brooking no delay—So never say No when Hope calls out—Come take the high way, MY way.

ALL CREATURES
GREAT AND SMALL

There is a sense in which we are all related to one another within the common framework of humanity, but that does not mean we are all alike in every way. The Creator in his infinite wisdom divided the world into separate races each with its own spiritual and physical possibilities and limitations. As they were all created may they all remain, each respecting the purity of his own race bound only by the things which unify and bless "all creatures that on earth do dwell."

We Cannot Always Understand

We cannot always understand why this or that should be. The picture Time is working out upon the tapestry is hidden on the other side and no one can explain the meaning of the heart-ache and the anguish and the pain.

Perhaps we never shall be told. Perhaps we'll never know. Faith must be sufficient as upon our way we go, never asking why hopes turned to ashes, joy to tears—believing that beyond the little measure of the years, we shall see the reason for the thing we suffered here. The answer will be given and God's purposes made clear.

All Our Days Are Numbered

*A*ll our days are numbered but it's not for us to know—just how many days are left. So don't let this one go—unmarked by something good or lovely, something true or fine—something that redeems it with a touch of the divine.

Think a thought that lifts your mind on to a higher track. Do the thing that takes a load from someone else's back . . . Say the word that changes conflict into harmony. Strike the note that turns the discord into melody.

Take this day out of its groove. Before you let it go—Give to it a meaning and a glory. Let it glow! There are many little ways in which it's possible—to sanctify the commonplace and make it beautiful.

Love Is A Solvent

*L*ove is a solvent. Love dissolves a heart as hard as stone. By a secret alchemy—by ways and means unknown—love works wonders—changing people, shaping lives anew—focusing a kindly light upon a hopeless view.

Love is a solvent. Love breaks up resentments firmly set. Love is the power that helps us to forgive and to forget—the grievances that rankle. Thoughts that hurt and things that smart. Love is the solvent that dissolves the hardness of the heart.

Christmas Is For Everyone

Christmas is for everyone for Christmas is for sharing—the joys, the blessings and the burdens. Christmas is for caring—putting into practice what the Saviour came to prove: that life is good when hearts are moved by kindness and by love.

Christmas is for everyone for Christmas is for spreading—the happy news from Bethlehem, the light of heaven shedding—on the vicious and the vile, the evil and the wrong. Christmas bids us stand and listen to the angel's song.

Christmas is for everyone; for every race and nation—bringing hope and happiness, redemption and salvation. Not for Christmas only but for all the world to see—God appearing in the vesture of humanity.

The Command

*P*eace! Be still—the Master said. We tend to think that He—spoke in soft and gentle manner—speaking tenderly—but was not this imperative, a definite command, a sharp rebuke to those who could not grasp or understand the meaning of the truths that He had come here to declare? Stop worrying. He says to us. Stop rushing here and there. Stop arguing. Stop quarrelling—and be not torn apart. Let the Word of God be heard within the quiet heart.

In this age of strife and noise and turmoil we today—need to listen for that voice—to hear and to obey . . . above the voices of the world that clamour hard and shrill—He speaks with calm authority, commanding Peace—Be still!

The Precious Portion

Do not think of life in terms of trial and tragedy, but simply as a tiny fragment of Eternity where we catch the echoed music of unfinished themes and strive with broken threads to work the tapestry of dreams.

In this world of change and chance we cannot hope to see the meanings and the purposes behind the mystery. Here we make beginnings but we cannot see the ends. Well contented we should be if when the dark descends, we can offer a thanksgiving unto One above for the blessings of the years: the happiness, the love, the precious portion granted. Let the rest be cast aside. Remember what a good God gave and not what was denied.

Heaven

*H*eaven is love made perfect within God's gracious plan. Heaven is love completed beyond life's little span. Heaven is love's true homeland where kindred souls abide—where death has no dominion and nothing can divide.

Heaven is love's tomorrow, unmarred by doubt or fear. Heaven is where we harvest the seed we scatter here. Heaven is love's fulfilling the promises made good—of all that we have dreamed of but never understood.

Nine Times Out Of Ten

Nine time out of ten life seems to work out for the best. Nine times out of ten you find that if you let things rest—Providence will sort them out without your helping hand—Not perhaps exactly in the way that you had planned—but in a wiser way and from a broader point of view. So do not try to force events or push your own plans through . . . Cease to worry. Trust and pray. Though things look black as night—Nine times out of ten you find that everything comes right.

Follow Me

Never heed the sceptics or the cynics who deny—truths that have withstood the storms of ages rolling by . . . They who doubt the Word of God have nothing to replace—the wisdom, the philosophy, the glory and the grace—of the Truth proclaimed to man in little Galilee—Valid for the passing needs of every century.

Times may change as change they must, but Truth can never be—subject to the fads and fashions of humanity . . . Truth eternal shines above the turmoil and the strife—in the form of One who was Himself the Way, the Life.

None before or since has said the things He came to say. He spoke for future generations and for this, our day . . . when He taught upon the hills and preached beside the sea—the simple gospel of the Kingdom saying, Follow Me.

Under The Shadow Of A Guiding Hand

We do not always see the way ahead. We do not always know which path to tread. This is the point at which we need to light the lamp of Faith to take into the night.

Trust and believe that God is leading you to a fulfilment hidden from your view. Know only good can come of what is planned, under the shadow of that guiding Hand.

It is not always granted us to see what lies behind the present mystery. Waste not your words in asking why or where. Time will unfold the answer to your prayer.

All Things New

Newness of life may the New Year bring—
New life for every living thing—Man and beast
and soil and tree—languish in their impurity . . .
The earth is sick and sour and old—The world's
long tale is all but told—but the Leader rides on
through the storm and the strife—saying, "I am
the Way, the Truth and the Life."

We who are willing lost paths to retrace—how
can we rescue the whole human race? We, the
believers, how can we restore—the faithless, the
hopeless who cry at the door? . . . The promise
still holds and the promise is true—"Behold,"
said the Lord, "I make everything new."

QUIET TIMES

Quietude is not a frilling to mental composure. It is a necessity. Unless the mind is at ease it cannot make contact with that other world which is the fountain of all inspiration.

Echoes In A Quiet Room

I sit in a web of shadows—and the clock in sleepy mood—wakens the sense of magic that comes with solitude . . . I hear—or I dream I'm hearing beyond its fairy chimes—the echo of lost enchantments, and music of gracious times.

The whisper of silks and satins. The tones of an old spinet. The footsteps of stately figures, dancing a minuet . . . The tinkle of crystal glasses. The laughter, like silver bells. The voices as soft and lovely as murmur of waves in shells.

The swish of a fan unfolding. The clink of a jewelled chain. You ask is it fact or fancy. The mystery must remain . . . I and the clock know the answer, but the secret we must keep. We know what we hear in the stillness when the old house falls asleep.

The Quiet Ways

Whether you are sitting by a well, wandering round an old church or walking in deep lanes you are going in the right direction if it is peace you are seeking. We do not realise it because we live in a bedlam of noise these days, but deep inside we are all longing for peace because we have lost it. There is something within that is crying out for quietness because we need it. You are not alone in this desperate need. At every turn you will meet one with whom you can claim a relationship. Life on its present levels degrades us. Join then the ranks of those who are going about in this depraved world hungry for a peace that is a spiritual food for famished souls.

Down In The Secret Garden

Year by year the blackbird comes the April nest to build. Year by year the little sunken garden here is filled—with liquid notes that rise and fall like fountains through the trees—in a jet of silvery music blowing on the breeze.

Deep below the street it lies, this narrow walled-in place—and upon the moss green stones the shadows interlace—when boughs of apple and of lilac in the wind are stirred . . . Year by year it comes, the magic fluting of this bird—down there in the secret garden somewhere out of sight—in the morning glory and the mellow evening light.

Lost In A Crowd

When many faces I can see—I'm lost in multiplicity. And losing my identity I ask in terror, Where is me? The I that hides in flesh and bone—is blind and deaf when not alone.

When many voices can be heard—crescendo, rising word on word—I cannot hear the voice that calls—in solitude when silence falls . . . For only there is wholeness found—beyond the range of sight and sound—the integrated self is free—to come and go, to hear and see.

The Day Of The Pearl

Now, and then you live a day outside the daily round—Chains are loosed, old concepts die, a different world is found—New dimensions open, joy is glimpsed, perfection seen—Like a peep of paradise flashed out upon a screen.

You were given eyes to see and thoughts to understand—Someone else's self-made garden wonderfully planned—Woke a sleeping dream in you that will forever be—Like a pearl encapsulated in a memory.

Go With The Flow

Go with the flow of Providence wherever that may be. Go with the current that knows its way into the open sea . . . Don't stand about on the brink of life afraid to venture in. Go with the flow of circumstances. Follow the voice within.

Go where God wills although it leads to stress and turbulence—Go with the driving of the wind that moves the day's events . . . Go where you're driven. Trust the hand that will not let you go— pulled by the tides, you know not where, but going with the flow:

Be Still And Listen

*H*ow can He come to an unquiet mind? How show His face to the inwardly blind? How can a sense of His presence be caught—in the confusion of turbulent thought?

If you would savour the calm of that peace—stop, wait and listen. Let questionings cease. Sit in the silence. Be still and believe—that you at His hands a great gift will receive—of healing and blessing . . . Doubt not He will come—as once to the lame and the deaf and the dumb—He came with new life—to revive and restore. Make ready your heart for He stands at the door.

Sit By The Well

Crowds had thronged with their demands—eager for those healing hands—and so when evening shadows fell—the Master came to Jacob's Well—to sit awhile and to refresh—the weariness of mind and flesh.

If He, the Lord, desired to rest—we too when troubled and hard-pressed—should learn of Him and drop the load—to rest awhile beside the road.

Sit by the well. You've travelled far. There is no well? Then where you are—Repose in Him that you might live—and living water He will give—your thirst to quench when strength has gone. Replenished, you can travel on.

Take Your Time

*T*ake your time—or time takes you and drains your strength away. Take a minute, maybe two, throughout your busy day—for slowing down to meditate—from wordly things apart—in a quiet place to wait with a receptive heart. Take your time to think about the greatest things of all— take your time to work it out before the curtains fall.

Why the worry? What's the hurry? Take your time and stroll—picking from life's wayside hedges that which feeds the soul . . . Take your time and walk on grass; to look at flowers and trees—wandering and pondering on wonders such as these . . . Slacken pace to see the view. Take your time or time takes you.

Believing

Don't go round looking for sympathy, displaying your weakness for others to see . . . Trust not on luck, it's a trick and a fake—but build up a spirit that nothing can break.

Believe in yourself and the Other who's there—Holding you close in His own special care . . . Face every day with clean hands and clean slate. It's never too soon and it's never too late. To shoulder your burden and make a new start—with a song in your soul and a hope in your heart.

The Right Word For Today

When you feel frustrated, helpless and distraught—with the many battles that daily must be fought—Quietly sit and lower your rope into the well—of life that is as high as heaven and as deep as hell.

Each must draw his bucket of water, foul or pure—each must choose things good or evil, flimsy or secure—Each must make his choice: Life's law to flout or to obey—to be dumb or to proclaim the right word for today.

A GOOD NEIGHBOUR

Fortunate are you if you know what it is to have a good neighbour. Fortunate indeed if you can go away for a long time or a little secure in the knowledge that there is someone next door who will keep a watchful eye on cat, garden, and property while you are away. If you have a good neighbour you are on the way to having a good friend.

Neighbour and Friend

*S*he watches when she knows that there is nobody about. She wonders when strangers click the gate, passing in and out . . . She keeps a caring eye on things; concerned, she is aware—of anyone or everyone who has no business there.

Conscious of her duty as a neighbour, standing guard—Observing the comings and goings from a window or a yard.

Fortunate are they in whom these two great virtues blend—the capacity of being both a neighbour and a friend.

330

Let Hope Go Ahead

Let Hope go ahead and you follow. Let Hope go before you today. Things will be better tomorrow if Hope be in view all the way—for Hope bears no load on her shoulders—Smoothing the rocks and the ruts—she forces a path through the boulders, dismissing the ifs and the buts.

You won't be afraid to keep going—where Hope sheds a gleam on the track—for Hope with her lamp brightly glowing—moves forward and never turns back . . . she never needs goading or prodding—unflagging she makes for the height—while you in her footprints come plodding—eyes fixed on her beautiful light.

Alone you would soon give up trying. Alone you would never succeed—but Hope undismayed and undying—strides forward to give you a lead . . . And now that a new year is dawning—and unknown the road you must tread—There's nothing to fear if each morning—you're willing to send Hope ahead.

So Little

*T*he gentle smile, the reconciling touch—can cost so little and can mean so much—to heal a breach or mend a friendship broken—a letter written, or a sentence spoken.

What hurts and pangs we suffer needlessly! What pains inflict, because we cannot see—how much we lose through conflicts and contentions—poisoning life with quarrels and dissensions.

Let them all go and love triumphant be—over all evil, hate, greed, jealously . . . Love's tender word, forbearing and forgiving—brings to the heart true peace and joy of living.

Time Steps Out

*T*ime is slow when we are young, but as the years proceed—Time steps out and seems to move at twice its former speed . . . Swiftly are the milestones passed—we see them flashing by— Quickly do the birthdays come—Time races . . . seasons fly.

Do not bank upon the future—It's not yours to plan—No one but your Maker knows the measure of your span . . . We should always live each day as if it were the last—the only chance to make amends for failings of the past.

The Backlash

Nature always lashes back. Man never really wins—so we have to pay the price for all the many sins—of ignorance and arrogance that we commit each day—all because we will not live the good, the simple way.

We pollute the rivers and contaminate the seas—and with deadly poisons spread the earth and spray the trees—We create obnoxious waste and dump it anywhere. We make fumes that load with death the sweetness of the air.

Faster we desire to turn the wheels of industry—in the sacred name of progress and prosperity—Let us learn before our follies bring on us the curse—of Him whose everlasting laws sustain the universe.

Three Days

*T*hree days and three days only are really your concern—So drop the futile worries and let the seasons turn . . . Three days! You'll find it simpler reducing things this way—to yesterday, tomorrow and the present day.

The first you cannot alter for yesterday has gone—and though regrets still linger you have to carry on—praying for forgiveness—There's nothing else to do—to banish the remembrance of all that troubles you.

Tomorrow is a secret. The far horizon's rim—conceals God's hidden purpose—so leave it all with Him. Today's the day that matters. Today is yours to live—So take it and be grateful for what it has to give.

Too many

*T*oo many people—too many crowds—too many babies born. Too many houses where there should be—cattle and crops and corn . . . . Too many voices—seldom a pause—making a restful space. Too many noises jarring the ear. Never a quiet place.

Too many smashes—too many cars. Not enough time to reflect. Too many clashes—too many words. Too many marriages wrecked . . . Too many homes where Love is left out. Homes rich and poor where you see—selfishness, cruelty, strife, discontent. Hell where a heaven should be.

This is our world as created by man—Man who has marred the original plan—spoiling the earth that the Saviour once trod—trying and failing to live without God.

The Kindred Spirits

Kindred spirits meet unsought—By the alchemy of thought. Towards each other they are led—guided by the unseen thread—of accident or passing chance—caught in webs of circumstance.

Kindred spirits, souls in tune—come together late or soon—like notes that harmonize when played. Thus true marriages are made—and lifelong friendships come about. Time alone can work it out.

Surely there must be a force—behind all human intercourse—weaving lives through chance and change—the perfect pattern to arrange—so two in tune at last will meet—knowing life to be complete.

Pick and Choose

*P*ick and choose between the thoughts that throng around your mind. Some are good and some are bad, some happy, some unkind. But it's up to you to say which ones you'll entertain of the many thoughts that seek admittance to your brain . . . And remember thoughts have power to heal or to destroy—turning heaven into hell or sorrow into joy.

Thoughts can change life's colour, mould your face and change your views—so be careful what you think. You're free to pick and choose—so choose a good thought for the day, a thought to carry you—through the many problems that are bound to get at you—out there in the world where all is turmoil, strain and stress—Yours the choice so choose the best. Choose peace, choose happiness.

Things Change

When you get to the end of your tether—and your energy seems to have gone—When you're weary and wondering whether its worth while to keep struggling on—When the fire has gone out of your spirit—and your armour has fallen apart—Let go and let God do the fighting. Be still in your head and your heart.

When the music goes out of the morning and you cannot keep pace with the drum—When the flowers in the garden stop smiling—and the birds do not sing when you come . . . When the sun never peeps through your window and you look for the rainbow in vain—Ask someone to help and to heal you. Let Him take the brunt and the strain.

When you get to the end of your courage—and there's nothing much more you can do—Try folding your hands for a moment and letting God's guidance get through . . . Life can't be altered by worry. Stop trying to push it your way. Just let the good Lord take over. You'll find that things change when you pray.

Rich Man's Fare, But Table Bare

You can't afford this and you can't afford that—The bills must come first so you can't have the hat . . . That's life as we know it. You can't keep afloat—but remember your neighbour is in the same boat.

When we were young we weren't scrambling to reach—the top of the tree for the pear or the peach. We did not fight for the sweetest and best—grateful we were for the least we possessed.

That's why the children grow up as they do—not taught to look for the good and the true . . . Teachers and parents the guilt now must share—for leaving the children a table that's bare.

THE SPECIAL
FRIEND

*Sometimes in the course of life a mere
relationship can ripen into real friendship.
It can happen in a day or after a long period
of time, but you will know when it has
come. Your heart will tell you.*

The Keynote

A tuning fork will strike the note from which you take the key—for the making of the music of the melody . . . It cannot sound a range of tones and semi-tones for you. One note and one alone it strikes, but that one note is true.

Love is like a tuning fork that gives the note we need—for making life harmonious in thought and word and deed: the note we have to strike before we find the magic key—in which to play the music of the daily symphony: the symphony of living: blended themes that rise and fall. Sweet the sound if Love be found, the keynote of it all.

Time Was Kinder Than I Thought

*T*ime was kinder than I thought, the many changes that it wrought and the sorrows that it brought, proved at last beneficent. Time indeed was provident.

Much it took but much remained. Much was lost but more was gained. In ways that never were explained, the burden lifted from my back, the mountain moved, the cloud rolled back.

The dream that seemed impossible came true as by a miracle, through happenings most wonderful—I found the blessing that I sought . . . Time was kinder than I thought.

The New

*T*he New is here at your very door demanding to come in. You have heard it knocking. You have barred yourself within—and you have refused to answer. But the New is here bringing tomorrow, bringing the future, bringing another year.

A stranger, yes, but one with claims that cannot be denied, one you dare not leave unheeded in the dark outside, one to whom some day, somewhere, a hand you must extend, one who in the course of time may prove to be a friend.

Lord, This Day I Need Thee

Lord, this is a special time for me. And more than human love and sympathy—I need the comfort of the consciousness—that Thou art nigh to strengthen and to bless.

Lord, I've never come this way before. I need Thy Word my courage to restore . . . I need Thy hand to reach for fearlessly—in the ordeal that lies ahead of me.

Now in my weakness, Lord, I need so much—the balm and the blessing of Thy healing touch . . . Thee I have failed—and yet I dare to say—Be Thou my Friend and meet my need this day.

That Is What It Means To Have A Friend

Someone to tell your troubles to when troubles come along. Someone with whom to talk things over when they're going wrong. A prayer to say, a smile to give, a helping hand to lend—that is what it means to have a friend.

Someone to reinforce your courage when it starts to flag. Someone to ease the burden when the spine begins to sag. Someone to keep you going when a mountain you ascend—that is what it means to have a friend.

Someone to share the problem and to help you work it out. Somebody to confide in when assailed by fear or doubt. Someone to give you back your faith when hope comes to an end—that is what it means to have a friend.

Nobody knows

Nobody knows what a prayer can do—when somebody, somewhere, prays for you. Burdens are lifted and doors unbarred. Nothing seems quite so bad or hard.

Nobody knows how God intervenes—working His wonders behind the scenes, turning the evil away from us, in a way most marvellous.

Clearing a path through the tangled track. Easing the strain on the breaking back. When Hope fades away and is lost to view—Nobody knows what a prayer will do.

Every Day, Every Year

You need every friend you can make—in a world where things hurt, and hearts break. Friends who will always be there—the good and the bad times to share . . . But friendship two-sided must be—each giving much, yet both free—going a separate way—wherever life leads day by day.

Friendships, the new and the old—form links that connect and will hold—in spite of the day to day strain—One friendship will always remain . . . Through changes and chances you learn—To this one special friend you can turn—the friend who unchanged will appear any time—any day—any year.

Somebody Said That Somebody Said

Somebody said that somebody said. Trouble was caused and suspicion fed. Somebody passed on an idle word. Someone repeated what someone had heard.

There has been many a broken heart. Many a marriage has come apart. Many relationships have been changed. Many a neighbour become estranged. In many a home where peace once reigned affection and loyalty have been strained, and many a life is incomplete all because someone was indiscreet.

Many a friendship has been wrecked— through gossip unfounded and unchecked. Mischief was made and a rumour spread. Somebody said that somebody said.

Where Is Comfort

Who can face without defeat the worst that life can do—standing unembittered and unbroken? Who comes through—with faith undimmed the agonies of Love's most grievous loss? He who down upon his knees can look up at the Cross.

All around him others go to pieces hopelessly—underneath the bludgeonings of trial and tragedy—but they that wait upon the Lord their failing strength renew—knowing that His word is valid and his promise true . . . Where is solace?

Where is peace, the touch that cures and calms? Only in the comfort of the Everlasting Arms.

A Word Of Thanks

Words are so inadequate our feelings to convey. When the heart is full we often find it hard to say—how much we appreciate what other people do, but I hope these lines express my gratitude to you—for your friendship, for your help and for your sympathy—You will never ever know how much you've done for me . . . When I needed someone you were there to help me through—So these simple words of thanks I'd like to send to you: brief they are but truly meant—and with warm affection sent.

That Wonderful Day

*T*he wonderful day I shall never forget—That day long ago when we two met—Time stood still for a moment or two—when you saw me and I saw you.

Love at first sight. It happened thus—It happened that day and happened to us—strangers. Your name I'd never heard—We gave no sign and spoke no word.

It was nothing less than a miracle—impossible, incredible—To be in a strange and crowded place—becoming aware of a single face.

Who can explain it? Nobody—But it happened to you and it happened to me—in that first moment when we two met—on the wonderful day I shall never forget.

ODDS AND ENDS

After all, what does life consist of when all is said and done? Is it not a confusion of odds and ends, meetings and parting, failures and successes, beginnings and endings, bits and pieces. Make sure you make the most of the odds and ends that come your way. Each item has a meaning and a message, but it may take a lifetime to discover answers to the questions they raise.

Just For Fun

The sun like a crimson ball bounces amongst the trees—Here in the stormy twilight it comes rushing on the breeze—through the open gaps between the branches, running wild—Slipping up and dipping down like the plaything of a child.

The sun on such a day as this gets somewhat out of hand—Instead of holding court on the horizon, grave and grand—It abandons its dignity and frolics just for fun—forgetting it is King of the sky, His Majesty the sun.

The Last Leaf

*L*ook! Keep looking till it falls, the last leaf on the tree. When it flutters to your feet you'll know it cannot be—very long to wait until the winter's tale is told—with autumn's glory spent in piled up leaves, bronze, red and gold.

Look and keep on looking though the time you cannot spare—spare this, one moment more to stand, to wonder and to stare . . . This leaf you'll never see again; this autumn too must pass—unless reflected; given back through Memory's magic glass.

Which Way?

The season is passing by the door. So sparse is the summer's poor yield . . . The gold of the grain unharvested—lies wasted in the field.

Blame the rain. But first stand still. Consider Nature's laws. Against them all men have transgressed; so let us call a pause—and come to terms that satisfy the needs of all concerned. Things natural or mechanical? False doctrines have we learned?

The field beyond the meadow is an open book to read. Instead of sheaves the hayrick stands: a mocking joke indeed! Is this the way to treat the land? Is this the way to go—towards prosperity and peace? Ask them. They think they know.

You Know

You know that you are guided all the way. In the silence voices seem to say . . . This is the way; the only way for you. Trust it and take it, with the goal in view.

This is your road, the road of destiny. Trust and believe and protected you will be. Deep in the darkness through the night you grope—Over the hills of promise and of hope.

Keep to the track. Stray not to left or right. Keep bravely on and hold the end in sight. All will be well with Faith to point the way. There's glory ahead. Dawn ushers in the day.

That Second Chance

*E*very night that closes a day brings opportunity—to repent of the mistakes you made, and failed to see . . . At the time caught up in the confusions of the day—But now at last comes the quiet moment when you can pause to pray—for the second chance you want to do the thing that's right—feeling guilty you run in thought towards tomorrow's light.

We do not deserve that second chance, nor do we ever earn—the wages of our blessings. On we go but never learn—On we go still grasping out for what we think we need. Greedy for the gains of life . . . Ears deaf when others plead—For what you could supply . . . Night comes once more. Pay what you owe—Try again—then into tomorrow you can safely go.

The Benefit Of The Doubt

What does it matter after all what someone did or said?—Looking back it seems quite small when big things lie ahead—The unkind word should never ever be allowed to wreak—havoc in the home or heart, so think before you speak.

Does it really matter who was right or who was wrong—so long as relationships remain unbroken, just as strong—Never let a grievance fester. Draw the poison out—Give both enemy and friend the benefit of the doubt.

Somehow, Joy Comes Back

You thought you would never recover from the pain of a broken heart—when life's crystal bowl had been shattered—and the pieces flung apart.

But love has a sure way of dealing with human loss and lack . . . For time brings its own gentle healing—and somehow—Joy comes back.

The Rising Sun

Light precedes the rising sun that spreads a fiery fan—at the windows looking east where rays of glory span—the brightening horizon where the clouds gold-tipped make way—to prepare a royal welcome for the coming day.

We, too, should greet the sun's return as we would greet a king—for we know not what to us this new born day will bring . . . Blessed are we to stand and see' the splendour of its birth—bringing life and light unto the edges of the earth.

A New Face In The Looking-Glass

Money, time and trouble you expend upon the care—of yourself; the part you see, the skin, the hands, the hair . . . But what about the inner self, the part that's not on view—the brain, the mind, the heart—the other part, the other you.

If you spent more time in training thoughts to go the way—of kindness and unselfishness, your own small part to play—to make the world a better place—you'd soon begin to see—a new face in the looking glass, the you that you could be.

Christmas

Once again a song of joy resounds around the earth—the song that tells the wondrous story of the holy birth—of Him who made the worlds, the stars and every living thing. He, Redeemer and Messiah: Israel's promised King.

Christians, sing and sing again the song of Christmas Day—Tell the message of the angels and to all men say—Glory to God in the Highest, for the Christ is come to us—to proclaim a truth so simple, yet so marvellous.

Put the tawdry toys away. Let now your voice be heard—in praise of Him who was Himself the incarnated Word.

Time To Make Time

You make the time for making the pleasures you pursue—You make the time for taking the time it takes to do—the things that feed the ego and bolster up your pride—when the tiny whisper of conscience is denied.

But what time is devoted to inner questioning?—How many minutes do you spend on planning how to bring—something good to somebody struggling on their way—lightening the burden of someone's busy day?

Crossing Your Bridges

Never cross your bridges till the bridge comes into view. Never go to meet your problems. Wait a day or two—Circumstances change that rearrange the sorted pack. Never take a load before it's placed upon your back.

Half life's many miseries upon ourselves we bring—Yet how often comes along the unexpected thing . . . Trust not in yourself, clever tricks and common sense. Look beyond yourself and trust the ways of Providence.

Save!

*I*n these spendthrift extravagant days—We grope through a dark and crowded maze— Where moral values are cast aside—foundations crumble and subside . . . In former times we were told to save—what the hand of Providence gave. Spend is the order of today. But our fathers used to say—Save. Conserve. Redeem the past. To honest principles holding fast.

Let us resolve if given time—To purify this pit of crime. Rebuilding our once-loved land anew— on what is righteous, good and true—Saving the wreckage of the years—Saving with our toil and tears . . . Save the hedge, the tree, the lane— from vandal's hand and acid rain . . . save our souls and pray that we—discover our lost identity.

Little Parcels

*T*here's so much trouble in the world you often wonder why—some folks like to keep it brewing just to satisfy—selfish aims and petty minds, establishing the right—to keep the trouble on the boil, to argue and to fight.

Such a waste of precious time, when Time is on the move—and every moment brings a chance to learn and to improve—Self, self, self—how boring and how futile life must be—wrapped up in a little parcel labelled . . . All for me.

The Life-Saver

Can you bank on anything in these uncertain days?—Can you trust the word of him who deals in devious ways?—Dare you lean on promises that rest on quaking ground?—Would you place your faith in things unstable and unsound?

In this world of selfishness, of anarchy and crime—The wise reach for The Book that has withstood the test of time—The Book that spreads throughout the world the Law: God's golden rule—Life-line for the young, the old, the scholar and the fool.

Autumn

The first faint hint of what is yet to be—a pinkish tint upon the cherry tree—The old Virginia creepers turning red around the timbers of the garden shed—Lovely in its dying, yet how beautiful.—September's golden leaves: the autumn miracle.

As sure as clocks and calendars—the year when growing old—cloaks the woods in glory—bronze, crimson, amber, gold—The fires of Nature's making, the flames no man can stay: the mighty conflagration that runs from day to day—Like torches blaze the branches in wood and garden bower—September fades but not before it lives its finest hour.

Let Life Begin Anew

*E*very day that's granted you let life begin again. Do not cling to memories that leave a stab of pain. Never hold on to a grudge that rankles in the heart. Every day a new adventure and another start.

Never ruin in advance your chances of success—by brooding thoughts of failure and unhappiness. Don't invite more trouble if you want to get along—by constantly remembering the things that went all wrong.

Make amends for past mistakes while there is time to try. Do not leave it till tomorrow lest the chance slip by . . . Let the dawn ring up the curtain on a lovely view. Every day get up and say that life begins anew.

Index

Index